The
Ultimate
DOG
Quiz Book

TERESA SLOWIK

HOWELL
BOOK HOUSE
New York

Howell Book House
A Simon & Schuster Macmillan Company
1633 Broadway
New York, NY 10019

MACMILLAN is a registered trademark of Macmillan, Inc.

Library of Congress Cataloging-in-Publication Data
available on request

ISBN 1 87605 762 8

Printed and bound in Great Britain by
Caledonian International Book Manufacturing Ltd, Glasgow
10 9 8 7 6 5 4 3 2 1

CONTENTS

Acknowledgements

I wish to thank the American Kennel Club and the FCI for
permission to use their breed standards, publications, etc. I
would like to thank the many other organisations and
individuals who have helped with this book.

INTRODUCTION

A fascinating world filled with amazing characters, both human and canine, marvellous stories and heroic achievements. That is the World of Dogs.

There is so much history, so many incredible facts, such a vast body of work on the many breeds of dogs that make up the canine family. Now, for the first time, you have a chance to test your knowledge of dogs – in depth! Our questions – there are more than 1,500 of them – vary from the simple to the fiendishly testing.

Test your friends, your breed club or your training class by picking out a selection with varying degrees of difficulty. In general, you should score one point for each simple question, and one point for each part of a multi-part section. Where this rule is broken, as in the entertaining *Who Am I?* questions, then we explain what do do at the start of that section.

We hope you enjoy this trip down the path of dog knowledge – and we are pretty sure you'll discover some things you had never thought you would need to know!

CHAPTER ONE

General Questions

1. What is a pedigree or pure-bred dog?
2. What is a dog's pedigree or genealogy?
3. What is a breed standard?
4. What is meant by the term breed group?
5. What is the difference between a cross-bred dog and a mongrel?
6. What is a throwback?
7. What is a latch-key dog?
8. What is a feral dog?
9. What is a cur?
10. What is the name of the 1,200 mile sled race known as the last great race on earth, from Anchorage to Nome, Alaska?
11. Name one of two capital cities in the world where it is illegal to own a dog.
12. When is a couple not a couple but a brace?
13. What is a long dog?
14. What is meant by "Bought in utero"?
15. The French have an expression "humeur de dogue". What does it mean?
16. Which breed's name means "little captain" in Flemish?
17. Over what distance is the English Greyhound Derby run?
18. In England, a church or parish council often employed a dog-whipper. What were his duties?
19. What is a Dorgi? A Dalmatian-Corgi cross; a Dandie Dinmont-Corgi cross; or a Dachshund-Corgi cross.
20. What is the TROVAN system of identification for dogs?
21. What is meant by the term "dual purpose" dog.
22. What is cynology?
23. What is a Dam?
24. What is a Gusp?
25. What is a Sire?
26. What was a turnspit?
27. Which of the following countries has the highest percentage of dog owners: US, UK, Germany?

28. When would a dog be said to have a foul colour?
29. Hounds can be divided into 2 types. What are they?
30. A Draw has 2 meanings in field sports. Name one?
31. What is venery?
32. An old working terrier guide quotes "an inch per pound". What does it refer to?
33. What does downfaced describe?
34. In Elizabethan London, plays were banned on Thursdays, and the day was reserved for what dog-related sport?
35. In the 17th Century, Oliver Cromwell banned Christmas mince pies, dancing round the maypole, and the export of which breed of dog?
36. Families with children are twice as likely to have a dog than a household with no children. True or false?
37. What is a Galton whistle?
38. How many dogs are listed in the first British Stud Book? Is it 3189, 4027 or 6003?
39. What are Post Dogs?
40. What is Hound Trailing?
41. When are dogs shown on the flags?
42. When was the last wolf killed in Britain? Was it 1300, 1660 or 1785?
43. Which is the smallest recorded dog in the world? Is it a Yorkshire Terrier, a Maltese or a Bolognese?
44. The German Shepherd Dog is also known by what other name?
45. What were the Brown Dog Riots?
46. Which newspaper group sponsors the English Greyhound Derby?
47. Sniffer dogs are trained to search for drugs, people, and equipment. What other task have sniffer dogs been trained for in connection with the building trade?
48. What is a Halti collar?
49. What is meant by the term "Bandog"?
50. World Animal Day is an internationally recognised day commemorating what?
51. What is a canine biathlon?
52. What is a lurcher?
53. What is a "Bye" or "Bye-Dog"?

54. When would you describe a dog's coat as "blown"?

55. In greyhound racing in Britain, what is the colour of the jacket won by the dog in trap one?

56. In 1993, at the annual Cotswold Country Fair, an 18-month old lurcher made a record-breaking canine high jump over a smooth wooden wall. Was the height of the jump:-
    a.   3.58m (11ft 9in)
    b.   4.05m (15ft 9.5in)
    c.   3.72m (12ft 2.5in)

57. What is the greatest number of "Best in Show" awards won by any individual dog in all-breed shows in the USA? Is it 175, 203 or 345?

58. What is the greatest number of Challenge Certificates (CCs) won in Britain by any dog? Is it 78, 88 or 98?

59. Can you name the dog that holds the record for greatest number of Challenge Certificate wins?

60. What is the largest recorded number of puppies born in a litter?

61. Which dogs hold the rank of honorary Sergeant Major, always wear their stripes on duty, and had a bounty price of $30,000 on their heads?

62. Which Spanish coin has the nickname "La perra chica" – the little dog?

63. What is "viola canina" more commonly known as?

64. What is a snap dog?

65. What type of dog is depicted on the Bayeux Tapestry?

66. In Elizabethan England, bear-baiting was a popular sport. How many mastiffs were regarded as a fair fight for a bear? Was it 4,6 or 8?

67. Horehound and Hound's-Tongue are plants which were used in a variety of herbal remedies. Which remedy required the leaves to be crushed with salt and applied to the affected part of the body?

68. Mandrake (Mandragora officinarum) is a plant closely related to deadly nightshade. It was used in witchcraft, as its fleshy and forked root resembled the human form. Gathering the root was regarded as dangerous, as it was believed that when the root was pulled from the ground it would shriek, and the gatherer was liable to madness or even death. What safe

method was developed to gather the root?

69. How did the dog rose (rosa canina) acquire its name?

70. At Christmas, why should you be careful when using poinsetta leaves, mistletoe berries, and christmas roses as decoration?

71. An Australian Cattle Dog called Bluey holds the record for being the oldest dog. How old was Bluey when he died in 1939? Was he 23, 27 or 29?

72. Which breed holds the record for siring the most number of puppies? Is it a Labrador Retriever, Border Collie or Greyhound?

73. What is the difference between the British Sporting Division and the American Sporting Group?

74. What do the initials DNF stand for?

75. Haw is a term usually associated with ectropion, meaning a drooping or sagging lower eyelid which shows an abnormally large amount of conjunctival lining. What is its other meaning when referred to in sled dog racing?

76. American Indians used dogs as draught animals, hauling loads on special 2-pole skin sleds. Can you name this type of sled?

77. Canadian Mounties started dog sled patrols in 1872. When were they replaced by snowmobile patrols? Was it 1969, 1974 or 1981?

78. Bandogges, tynkers and mooners were all 16th Century types of which dog? Was it hunting dogs, sheepdogs or watchdogs?

79. The Celtic word "Greg" or "Grech" simply means dog, but tradition has it that it is the origin of which breed name?

80. The oldest dog remains in Europe – "Senckenberg Dog" – were found near Frankfurt, Germany. Do they date from approx 2000 BC, 7538 BC or 9673 BC?

81. When coursing, when would a dog be described as "cute"?

82. What modern breed has its origin in the Bullenbeiser?

83. In February 1980, the Australian Post issued a series of 5 stamps as a tribute to the Australian dogs. The Australian Cattle Dog and the Australian Kelpie were featured. Can you name the other 3 breeds featured? (1 point for each correct breed).

84. Which is the official dog of the state of Maryland?

85. Name King Arthur's legendary dog.

86. The Israeli Air Force trained a dog to act as a co-pilot. True or false?

87. Name the dog that was the first American war dog to be awarded the Purple Heart and the Silver Star in World War II.

88. Which religious order were nicknamed the "domini canes" – "the hounds of the Lord" in the Middle Ages?

89. How many dogs sailed to America with the Pilgrim Fathers on the Mayflower in 1620. Was it 2, 5, or 7?

90. In ancient Roman law, dogs were classified as "ferae naturae" – wild animals, which meant that they belonged to whom ever took them. True or false?

91. In modern law, what is a dog classified as?

92. At what point does a dog's barking become a legal nuisance. Is it a frequency of 20, 30, or 40 barks per minute?

93. In which year was bull-baiting and dog fighting banned in Britain. Was it 1789, 1800, or 1835?

94. When was quarantine first introduced in Britain. Was it 1901, 1918, or 1947?

95. In many American states, dog licensing is compulsory for dogs over 6 months of age. Often fees are higher for what type of dog?

96. What are American "leash laws"?

97. In January 1991, the Royal Mail issued a set of special stamps commemorating 3 historic occasions.

    a.   The stamps commemorated the bicentenary of the Royal Veterinary College, the centenary of Crufts dog show, and what other event?

    b.   The 5 stamps featured dog paintings by which artist?

    c.   The 1991 stamps were the 2nd time that the Royal Mail issued a set of dog stamps. In which year was the previous set issued?

98. There are 4 main methods used to identify and mark individual dogs. Registration tags or medals are 1 method. Which are the other 3? (1 point per each correct answer).

99. a.   What is a "Truffleur"?

    b.   What is a truffle?

    c.   What animals are used for hunting truffles?

100. a. What award is commonly known as the "Animal V.C."?
    b. Who awarded it?
    c. Only 53 animals received this award. How many of them were dogs?

101. The dressmaker or tailor has a very wide range of material to work with, including some which have canine connections.
    a. Can you describe a dogstooth or houndstooth woven pattern?
    b. What is poodle cloth?
    c. What is bark crepe?

102. a. Where does Schutzhund originate?
    b. What does the word mean?
    c. What type of training is Schutzhund?

103. Peter Mayle in his book "Scruffs: the alternative dog show" lists the 5 different classes in which the judges assess the dogs' performances. These include disobedience, and aroma. Can you list the other 3 categories? (1 point per each correct answer).

104. a. If you were playing at dice and threw a "dog-throw" what would you have got?
    b. If you were then accused of "doggery" in the game, what would you have done?
    c. If your partners told you that you had "gone to the dogs" what would they mean?

105. It is a difficult day at school, and the teacher has told you off for a number of different reasons. What does the teacher mean by criticising the following?
    a. Dog Latin.
    b. Doggerel.
    c. What is the Dog-letter?

106. a. If you got into a fight, which was described as a "dogfight", what type of fight was it?
    b. During the fight, you suffer a "dog-fall", what happens?
    c. Once the fight is over, you decide that you would "lie doggo", what would you do?

107. a. If you were out hunting with a "lady pack", what would this be?

b.   If the pack was made up of "jelly dogs", what would they be?

c.   If the pack of hounds was chasing a "Jack", what would they be after?

108. The "hair of the dog" is a well-known phrase, which has had a variety of different meaning over the years.

a.   Originally "hair of the dog" was a medicinal cure. What was it meant to cure?

b.   It was later adopted as a cure for a drinking "hangover". What did the ancient Roman "hangover" recipe require you to do with the "hair of the dog"?

c.   What are the 3 main ingredients of the modern "Hair of the dog" hangover cure?

109. You are out having a meal in a restaurant, and the following items are on the menu.

a.   What is the main ingredient in Alsatian soup?

b.   What are Talahassee Hush Puppies?

c.   What is a "dog-in-a-blanket"?

110. a.   If you are going up a "dog-legged" staircase, what type is it?

b.   If you are travelling in a "dogcart", what type of vehicle is it?

c.   If you are out watching a sun-dog, what are you be looking at?

CHAPTER TWO

Breed Questions

The following questions deal specifically with individual breeds, and are divided into 6 sections, ranging from simple through to complex questions, requiring good breed knowledge.

Section 1

111. Which breed is often known as "The Bobtail"?
112. Which Italian breed has a corded coat?
113. What is a black and white, or a blue and white Great Dane called?
114. Which breed was originally known as "Round-headed Bull and Terriers", or "Bullet Heads"?
115. Which is the national dog of Finland?
116. Which breed was used as a carriage-dog, and a fire-engine dog?
117. Which breed has a lamb-like appearance?
118. Which is the largest of the Terrier breeds?
119. Which breed is known as the poor man's racehorse?
120. A Caniche is known in English as which breed?
121. Name a French gundog which originated in Brittany.
122. Name a French hound which originated in Brittany.
123. Which breed is the smallest of the Hungarian sheepdogs?
124. Which breed is named after a provincial State in Mexico?
125. Which breed is often referred to as the aristocrat of the canine world?
126. Which breed was once described inaccurately as "the ugly and plebian Dutchman", but is in fact Belgian?
127. Beijing is the new name for the capital of China, but which breed is named after its original name?
128. The Arabs believe that one breed of dog is sacred as it was a gift from God. Which breed is it?
129. By which English name is the Schaeferhund known?
130. Which group of dogs contains the largest and the heaviest breeds?
131. Which breed had the nickname of "Charlie's Hope Terrier"?

132. Which breed should move with a hackney-like action?

133. When does a Dalmatian get its spots?

134. What colour should the coat of a Toy American Eskimo dog be?

135. Which breed moves with a characteristic bear-like gait?

136. What is Le Chien Ecureuil or Squirrel Dog better known as?

137. How should a Pug carry its tail?

138. The Dobermann's coat can be black, red, blue, and what other colour?

139. Which breed has the title of "King of the French hounds"?

140. The Japanese Chin is taller and heavier than a Pekingese. True or false?

141. In Europe, it is known as the Deutsche Dogge. What is the breed known as in Great Britain and America?

142. Does the Basenji bark?

143. Which breed of dog sings?

144. Which toy breed originates from Madagascar?

145. Which breed was the traditional gift of the Dalai Lama?

146. Which breed standard allows for a mollera, or open spot on the top of the skull?

147. Which is the game-keeper's night dog?

148. Which is Scotland's only national gundog?

149. Which is the heaviest and largest of the Setters?

150. Which breed is named after the capital of Cuba?

151. Which is the tallest of the Hound group?

152. Which breed is known as "the grey ghost"?

153. What was the Potsdam Greyhound?

154. By what other name is the Manchester Terrier known?

155. What is a pocket Beagle?

156. What is the King Charles Spaniel known as in America?

157. The native Inuit tribe bred a sled dog which has become popular throughout the world. What is it known as?

158. Which of the following hounds has a pronounced dewlap? Bloodhound, Basenji or Irish Wolfhound?

159. Which is the smallest of the German Spitz breeds?

160. Which breed of French hound is descended from the royal White hounds, and shares a name with a type of fine china?

161. Which breed of dog is named after the Hebrew name for Palestine?
162. Which breed is named after the German town of Rottweil?
163. Which breed was originally recognised as a Broken-haired Scotch Terrier?
164. Which working dog is named after a region of France famous for its cheese?
165. Which breed was developed by Nicholas Rose, the owner of the Cafe de Groenendael?
166. The Chinese Crested Dog comes in 2 varieties. The Hairless and the Powderpuff. What is the main difference between the two?
167. By what name is the Sloughi sometimes known?
168. Which country does the Sloughi originate from?
169. What are Laufhunds?
170. Which Japanese breed was bred for dog-fighting, and is the canine equivalent of sumo wrestlers?
171. Which breed is described as being "multo in parvo" – much in little?
172. What is the main difference between Cardigan and Pembroke Welsh Corgis?
173. Which working breed is claimed by both France and Belgium, and recognised by the FCI as Franco-Belgian?
174. Which was the Bedlington Terrier originally known as:- Roseneath or Rothbury Terrier?
175. What is an Armant?
176. Which breed is known as Diabletin Moustache – the moustached little devil?
177. The Lancashire Heeler and the Welsh Corgi were bred as cattle dogs. What was their role?
178. In Japan, when a baby is born the parents usually receive a present of a statue of which breed of dog, signifying health, happiness and a long life?
179. Which gundog has long ears, shaped like vine leaves?
180. What is a Briquet?
181. The Mexican Hairless lacks pre-molar teeth. True or false?
182. Bugeilei is Welsh for which breed of dog?
183. Which breed is nicknamed the "barking bird dog"?
184. Which two breeds have a coat which can be Isabella in colour?

185. What is a Blue Heeler?
186. Which breed is known in France as a Carlin?
187. The Abso Seng Kye, from Tibet, has a name which means Barking Lion Sentinel Dog. By which name is it better known?
188. Which is the smallest of the French Griffons of the Vendeen?
189. The majority of Japanese Chin coats are black and white in colour. True or false?
190. Which breed was saved from extinction by the Duke of Newcastle, and found royal favour with King Edward VII and George V? Is it the English Setter, the Clumber Spaniel or the Flat Coated Retriever?
191. Which breed was sometimes called the American Duck-Retriever?
192. Which Irish breed is nicknamed the "dare-devil"?
193. Which English breed is known as the Jones Terrier in America?
194. What is the modern equivalent of the medieval Sleuth or Slot Hound?
195. From which country does the Anatolian Shepherd (Karabash) Dog originate?
196. Which breed was developed to hunt wolves on the Russian steppes?
197. Which dog was originally developed as a fighting dog, and has a massive, loose wrinkly skin with harsh bristles, as a form of protection.
198. Which breed was originally known as the Dutch Barge Dog when first introduced into Britain?
199. Which is the smallest type of Pekingese?
200. What is a black and white Newfoundland called?
201. What is a Grig or Her-Hound?
202. Which breed was described in the sixteenth century as a "comforter"?
203. What is a kangeroo hound?
204. Which British Foxhound has a rough coat?
205. How many types of Fox Terrier are there?
206. Is the Australian Silky Terrier another name for the Australian Terrier, or are they separate breeds?

Breed Questions

207. What is the official name of the Red Setter?
208. Is there such a breed as a Golden Labrador?
209. Which country is the home of the Kelpie?
210. Which breed was originally introduced into Britain as the Shan Dog?

Section 2

211. Which of the Bichon breeds is the only one with a double coat?
212. The Staffordshire Bull Terrier has a low-set tail, which has been described as looking like an old-fashioned pump handle. True or false?
213. What is special about a Tibetan Terrier's feet?
214. The Working, Waterside or Bingley Terrier was developed in the river valleys of the Colne, Calder, Warfe and Aire. What has the breed become known as?
215. Which breed has a coat which is described as dead grass in colour?
216. The Bulldog has a particularly characteristic gait. What is special about it?
217. What type of eye should a Dobermann have?
218. The Portuguese Water Dog has a double waterproof coat. True or false?
219. Bearded Collies are born black, blue, brown or fawn, with or without white markings. True or false?
220. Which German breed was developed in the 1840's, to embody the characteristics of the heraldic dog featured in the town's crest?
221. "Huddersfield Ben" is regarded as the father of which breed?
222. What do the Newfoundland, Chesapeake Bay Retriever and the Irish Water Spaniel have in common?
223. Can you name the breed of dog whose name is Norman French for a hunting dog, and was a term used in Britain until the mid-18th century as a collective name for all hunting dogs?
224. In 1896, at the Berlin Dog Show, the smooth and wirehaired versions of a breed were separated. Which were the 2 breeds?

225. Which breed was first exhibited in Germany as the Russian Bear Schnauzer?
226. Which breed of dog was adopted as the state dog of Louisiana?
227. With which breed is the colour Belton associated, and what is it?
228. When may a Staffordshire Bull Terrier's eye rims be pink?
229. Why is the Cardigan Welsh Corgi known as the "yard-long dog"?
230. Which breed was originally known by a variety of names including Poltalloch and Roseneath Terriers, before being first classified by its present name in 1904?
231. What is special about a Puli's coat colour?
232. Was the American Cocker Spaniel's breed standard originally defined by weight or by height?
233. Which of the spaniel breeds has a top-knot coming down between the eyes into a widow's peak?
234. What is the ideal Boston Terrier expression?
235. What is a Boxer's cushion?
236. Which breed was first exhibited at the Birmingham Dog Show in 1860, and 4 dogs from the royal kennels were exhibited at Islington in 1869?
237. Which Dutch breed is named after the 18th century patriots – the Keezen, and became the mascot of the popular people's opposition party?
238. Annual contests are held to select the "King Barker" of which breed?
239. Which South American breed was used as an ancient hot-water bottle?
240. Would you have found a Dobermann being shown at a Victorian dog show?
241. Which terrier has a soft wavy coat, which does not moult, and which needs to be clipped?
242. Which is heavier the Maremma sheepdog or the Kuvasz?
243. Which breed has the head like a hippopotamus?
244. Which Italian gundog has 2 standards – show and working?
245. What are a Poodle's bracelets?
246. Which is the largest of the Retriever breeds?

247. The Scottish Deerhound has drooping hindquarters. True or false?
248. What are the only acceptable colours for a Flat-Coated Retriever?
249. What is the official name for the "Yankee Terrier"?
250. Which breed was nicknamed the "Black Satin Gentleman"?
251. How many native terrier breeds are recognised in Ireland?
252. The Welsh Springer Spaniel comes in a variety of colours, including liver and white, and black and white. True or false?
253. Which gundog has an otter tail?
254. The Bichon Frise has haloes of black or dark skin surrounding the eye, enhancing the expression. What colour must the eye rims be?
255. Which breed of sheepdog has the characteristic of "backing" – running over the backs of tightly herded sheep?
256. What is a Xoloitcuintli?
257. Which of the 4 varieties of Belgian Shepherd Dog has a short coat?
258. Who or what is the "White Cavalier"?
259. The Glen of Imaal Terrier is an Irish breed, named after a particular valley or glen. In which county is the glen of Imaal located?
260. The Staffordshire Bull Terrier should be light and rangy in the hindquarters. True or false?
261. Reputedly the only dog that went down with the sinking of the Titanic in 1912, and his owner sued for $1,500 in compensation. What breed was it?
262. The Hospice St Bernard no longer breeds St Bernards for rescue work in the Swiss mountains. Which breed is used instead?
263. Which breed has a double-jointed neck, and ears which are so high placed and forward that they can be almost closed to the front?
264. Scottish Terriers were originally grouped together, until 1873 when they were divided into which 2 separate classifications?
265. Which breed should have movement like "quicksilver",

allowing fast, rapid and sudden turns, abrupt stops, and springing starts?

266. What is the correct degree of slope in the shoulder blades of a Shetland Sheepdog?

267. Which sled dog was created to combine the speed of Huskies with the strength of the larger sled dogs?

268. What is the main difference between the Papillon and the Phalene?

269. Which continental terrier was recognised by the FCI in 1963, and has Scottish and Sealyham Terrier as a major part of its development?

270. The German Shepherd Dog's abdomen or underline must be clean and firm, and avoiding the tucked up appearance of the Greyhound. True or false?

271. Where does the Rafeiro do Alentejo come from?

272. Which breed has the head of a Bloodhound, the colouring of a Foxhound, and the legs of a Dachshund?

273. Which French breed is known for his "red stockings"?

274. How would you groom a Schnauzer coat?

275. What happens if an Afghan Hound is too straight at the shoulder?

276. Which breed was first exhibited as a Wire-haired Pinscher at the 3rd German International Show in Hanover in 1879?

277. In 1807, an English ship was wrecked off the coast of Maryland. The crew and 2 puppies were rescued, and tradition dictates that these 2 puppies were the originators of which breed?

278. Why did the Pug become the official dog of the Dutch House of Orange?

279. Which breed has a "kissing spot", and what is it?

280. Which breed has been described as "not bigger than common ferrets", or about the size of squirrels?

281. The West Highland White Terrier has front feet which are smaller than its hind feet. True or false?

282. What is meant by the term "Patou"?

283. Which is the fastest of the Scandinavian hounds?

284. When is a mincing step or gait permissible in Shetland Sheepdogs?

285. Which Tibetan breed should have a white spot on the chest,

which is a good luck sign signifying a brave heart?

286. In World War I, the German Army enlisted 48,000 dogs of one particular breed. Which was it?

287. The Bearded Collie has a very long silky coat which requires regular trimming. True or false?

288. What is a Billy?

289. When were the Cavalier and the King Charles Spaniels separated into 2 breeds? 1925, 1945 or 1965?

290. Which Australian breed was developed in the early 19th century from a cross between a smooth-haired merle Collie and the Dingo?

291. Where would you find a Schipperke's jabot?

292. The earliest known breed standard for the Borzoi was drawn up in the 17th century. True or false?

293. In Poland, the Lowland Sheepdog is divided into 3 sizes:- maly, sredni and duzy. Which size is the best known outside Poland?

294. The Cocker Spaniel was recognised as a separate breed in 1892. By what name was it known by in the show ring, prior to 1892?

295. In 1887, a Congress was held in Berne, Switzerland, at which an international breed standard was adopted. Which one?

296. The true or base colour of an Afghan Hound is considered to be found on which part of its body?

297. Which breed won BIS at Crufts in 1967, and BIS at the National Westminster Show, New York in 1968?

298. Beechgrove Will and Fansom were the first British Champions in which breed?

299. The Dandie Dinmont has a "digging front". Describe what this is?

300. The Curly-Coated Retriever was first shown at a British show in . . . 1860, 1870 or 1885?

301. Which Swedish breed is the heeler of the north?

302. Many of the early 17th century settlers at Jamestown, Virginia brought with them Bloodhounds. For what purpose were Bloodhounds used?

303. Which breed was first recognised in Britain and America in 1911, received its first Challenge Certificates at the Great

Joint Terrier Show in London, and has won BIS at the Westminster Show 4 times?

304. The Otterhound originates from which country?

305. Which was the first coonhound to be officially recognised in the United States?

306. What is a "July"?

307. Which of the following breeds has a tail known as a stern? Is it a Foxhound, Fox Terrier or Dalmatian?

308. Which breed has no undercoat, but either a short, bristly stand-off outer coat called a horse coat, or a slightly longer one called a brush coat?

309. Which was the first of the European all-purpose gundogs to be recognised in the United States?

Section 3

310. Which is the odd one out?
Cairn Terrier, Miniature Bull Terrier or Australian Silky Terrier.

311. Which is the odd one out?
Shar-Pei, Pekingese, or Shiba Inu.

312. Which is the odd one out?
Basenji, Saluki, or Rhodesian Ridgeback.

313. Which is the odd one out?
St Bernard, Collie, or Welsh Corgi.

314. Which is the odd one out?
Hungarian Puli, German Shepherd Dog, or Anatolian Shepherd Dog.

315. Which is the odd one out?
Harrier, Borzoi, or Ibizan Hound

316. Which is the odd one out?
Keeshond, Rottweiler or Pomeranian.

317. Which is the odd one out?
Tibetan Mastiff, Polar Bear or Chow Chow.

318. Which is the odd one out?
Lhasa Apso, Basset Hound or Elkhound

319. Which is the odd one out?
Siberian Husky, West Highland White Terrier, or Whippet.

320. Which is the odd one out?

Dandie Dinmont Terrier, Pug, or King Charles Spaniel.
321. Which is the odd one out?
Field Spaniel, Irish Water Spaniel, or Sussex Spaniel.
322. Which is the odd one out?
Norwich Terrier, Irish Terrier, or Welsh Terrier.
323. Which is the odd one out?
Bearded Collie, Kerry Blue Terrier, or Groenendael.
324. Which is the odd one out?
Italian Greyhound, Bolognese, or Maltese.

Section 4

The following questions deal with famous kennels associated with specific breeds. Can you match the following affixes or kennel names with the breed.

325. Of the Congo. Is it Basenji, Rhodesian Ridgeback, or Pharoah Hound?
326. Ormandy. Is it Petit Basset Vendeen, Affenpinscher, or Bull Terrier?
327. Munster. Is it Soft Coated Wheaten Terrier, Irish Terrier, or Kerry Blue Terrier?
328. Colonsay. Is it Scottish Terrier, Bedlington Terrier, or Norfolk Terrier?
329. Amherstia. Is it Greyhound, Saluki, or Whippet?
330. Sarona. Is it Greyhound, Italian Greyhound, or Saluki?
331. Diamond Hill. Is it Greyhound, Italian Greyhound, or Saluki?
332. Sulhamstead. Is it Irish Setter, Irish Wolfhound, or Irish Terrier?
333. Of Ware. Is it Sussex Spaniel, Welsh Springer Spaniel, or Cocker Spaniel?
334. O'Cloisters. Is it English Setter, Gordon Setter, or Irish Setter?
335. Banchory. Is it Labrador Retriever, Curly Coated Retriever, or Irish Water Spaniel?
336. Munden. Is it Labrador Retriever, Curly Coated Retriever, or Schnauzer?

337. Heather. Is it Scottish Terrier, Gordon Setter, or Bearded Collie?
338. Dandean. Is it Dandie Dinmont Terrier, Dobermann, or Schnauzer?
339. Ardagh. Is it English Setter, Pointer, or Sussex Spaniel?
340. De Fontenay. Is it Briard, Bouvier des Flandres, or Pyrenean Mountain Dog?
341. Barmere. Is it Boxer, Dachshund or Rottweiler?
342. Redgrave. Is it Mastiff, Bullmastiff, or Great Dane?
343. Rotherwoods. Is it Irish Wolfhound, Deerhound, or Greyhound?
344. Kennelgarth. Is it Scottish Terrier, Border Terrier, or Bedlington Terrier?
345. Wardrobes. Is it Bull Terrier, Boxer, or Beagle?
346. Tweedside. Is it Bulldog, Border Terrier, or Basset Hound?
347. Titlington. Is it Border Terrier, Borzoi, or Bloodhound?
348. Orchard. Is it Pekingese, Parson Jack Russell, or Poodle?
349. Breifny. Is it Welsh Terrier, Irish Water Spaniel, or Scottish Terrier?

The following affixes/kennel names are of historical breed importance, and are "protected" by being placed under the control of specific breed clubs. Can you match the following affixes with the appropriate breed.

350. Newmaidley. Is it Smooth Fox Terrier, Miniature Dachshund, or Pembroke Welsh Corgi?
351. Tundras. Is it Alaskan Malamute, Siberian Husky, or Samoyed?
352. Merryweather. Is it Miniature Dachshund, Miniature Poodle, or Miniature Schnauzer?
353. Piccoli. Is it Italian Spinone, Bracco Italiano, or Poodle?
354. Knockalla. Is it Glen of Imaal Terrier, Irish Red and White Setter, or Kerry Blue Terrier?
355. Portholme. Is it Lakeland Terrier, Border Terrier, or Skye Terrier?
356. Underbridge. Is it Kerry Blue Terrier, Staffordshire Bull Terrier, or Sealyham Terrier?

Breed Questions

357. Rooftreetops. Is it English Setter, Golden Retriever, or Pointer?
358. Redesgarth. Is it Basenji, West Highland White Terrier, or Rough Collie?
359. Benhooks. Is it Bulldog, Boston Terrier, or French Bulldog?
360. Addleston. Is it Deerhound, Borzoi, or Saluki?
361. Skibbereen. Is it Griffon Bruxellois, Affenpinscher, or Bichon Frisé?
362. Felsholt. Is it Cairn Terrier, Newfoundland, or Whippet?
363. Deepridge. Is it Rhodesian Ridgeback, Afghan Hound, or Whippet?
364. Waterside. Is it Lakeland Terrier, Yorkshire Terrier, or Airedale Terrier?
365. Culzean. Is it Chesapeake Bay Retriever, Golden Retriever, or Hungarian Vizsla?
366. Branston. Is it West Highland White Terrier, Cairn Terrier, or Dandie Dinmont Terrier?
367. Barchester. Is it Foxhound, Otterhound, or Bloodhound?
368. Wribbenhall. Is it Field Spaniel, Old English Sheepdog, or Manchester Terrier?
369. Nostrebor. Is it Norwich Terrier, Pomeranian, or Cocker Spaniel?
370. Touvere. Is it German Spitz, Belgian Shepherd Dog, or Bernese Mountain Dog?
371. Wolfox. Is it Wirehaired Fox Terrier, Finnish Spitz, or Hungarian Vizsla?
372. Bingley. Is it Airedale Terrier, Fell Terrier, or Australian Terrier?
373. Pennard. Is it Harrier, Brittany, or Golden Retriever?
374. Robqwen. Is it Welsh Springer Spaniel, Cardigan Welsh Corgi, or Welsh Foxhound?

Section 5

The following questions are multi-part, comprising 3 sections. Scoring is 1 point per correct answer to a maximum of 3 points.

375. a. What distinctive characteristic does the Rhodesian Ridgeback have?
b. Name one other breed which shares this characteristic?
c. Where does the Phu-Quoc originate from?

376. a. Which breed is named after the Norwegian city of Halden?
b. What type of dog is it?
c. It is the largest of the 4 recognised Stovare breeds. Can you name 2 others?

377. a. What is the smooth-coated Belgian Griffon called?
b. The smoothcoated Griffon type can largely be traced back to the use of which breed which was crossed with the Griffon?
c. What were the original Belgian street dogs called?

378. The FCI divides Griffon Bruxellois or Belgian Griffons into 3 breeds. What are they? (1 point per each correct answer).

379. a. The French developed the Basset varieties for slower, closer hunting. What is the German contribution to this type of hunting?
b. What is the German term for a Dachshund?
c. How are Dachshunds varieties divided in Germany?

380. It is particularly desirable for a German Shepherd Dog to have a complete dentition, as this will help the dog to have a powerful bite.
a. Which teeth can be missing before the lack of teeth is regarded as a serious fault?
b. In Germany, if more than 1 of these teeth is missing, what certificate is withheld?

c.   How many missing teeth are necessary to prevent a dog from entry in the S.V. Stud Book?

381. The Belgian Shepherd Dogs come in 4 varieties or types, differing in coat and colour.
a.   What is the name of the black, long-haired type?
b.   Which type has a fawn, coarse-haired coat?
c.   Which type has a fawn, short-haired coat with a black mask?

382. a.   When did the Golden Retriever receive official recognition in Britain? Was it 1895, 1913 or 1928?
b.   In 1936, the British Golden Retriever breed standard was revised to include another colour?
c.   In which countries in this colour still not undesirable?

383. a.   Which breed answered to the name of Toonie? Is it the Irish Setter, Rough Collie or the Shetland Sheepdog?
b.   What does Toonie mean?
c.   When was the breed recognised in Britain?

384. Which type of French Hound is available in 4 different sizes, and can you name 2?

385. a.   The King Charles Spaniel (English Toy Spaniel) and the Cavalier King Charles Spaniel come in a variety of different colours, i.e. white, tan and black variety. Name the other 3 colour types?
b.   What is the white, tan and black variety known as in GB?
c.   What is the white, tan and black variety known as in the US?

386. a.   What is the distinguishing feature between the Norfolk and the Norwich Terrier?
b.   When were the breeds separated in Britain? Was it 1925, 1947 or 1964?
c.   When were the breeds separated in the US? Was it 1925, 1979 or 1982?

387. a.   Which is the tallest of the following breeds:-
Alaskan Malamute, Siberian Husky or Eskimo dog.
b.   Which is the heaviest of the following breeds:-
Siberian Husky, Eskimo Dog or Samoyed.
c.   Which the lightest of the following breeds:-
Alaskan Malamute, Siberian Husky or Samoyed.

388. Mastiff-type dogs are found in many different countries.
What is the official name of the following:-
a.   Brazilian Mastiff.
b.   French Mastiff.
c.   English Mastiff.

389. a.   By what other names is the Lowchen known as?
b.   The Lowchen is usually clipped into a traditional cut.
What is it called, and can you describe it?
c.   What type of coat does the Lowchen have?

390. Malta is regarded as the home of many different breeds.
a.   What is the Melita known as in Britain?
b.   What is the Maltese Pocket Dog better known as?
c.   What is the Maltese Rabbit Dog?

391. a.   For which sport were Borzois originally bred?
b.   In the traditional hunt, Borzois worked in pairs. What 2
criteria were used to match the dogs?

392. Throughout the history of field sports, changing gun
technology has effected the type of gundog used in the field.
a.   When muzzle-loading guns were in use, there was a
need for patient and stationary gundogs. Which breed was
developed?
b.   When faster breech-loading guns were developed,
which type of dog was needed?
c.   Springer Spaniels were traditionally used to "spring"
the game, causing the birds to take to the air. What were the
spaniels often known as?

393. Different types of gundog have different ways of working in

the sporting field. How do the following work?
a. Retrievers?
b. Pointers?
c. Spaniels?

394. a. How many varieties of German Spitz are recognised by the FCI?
b. Which 2 varieties are recognised in the UK?
c. The largest variety of the German Spitz is called the Wolfspitz. Which Dutch breed is regarded as the German Wolfspitz's cousin?

395. a. Which breed did the Rev. John Russell develop in the mid-19th century?
b. For what purpose was the breed developed?
c. The name now covers different types of the breed. Which is the variety recognised in the UK?

396. The Portuguese Water Dog was developed to work with fishermen, and is a proficient swimmer. Name the 3 ways in which he earned his keep.

397. a. Which breed has a forehead which forms a distinct stop with the topline of the muzzle, but must not be forced back into the forehead like that of a Bulldog?
b. Which breed had its first show classes in 1895, at the St Bernard Club's Show in Munich?
c. The Boxer breed standard was first drawn up in 1896, and was based on the top dog at the First Boxer Speciality Show. Name the dog on which the breed standard was based?

398. a. Which Irish breed is known locally as the Rossmore Setter?
b. Apart from coat colour, can you name 2 other differences between the Irish Setter and the Irish Red & White Setter?

399. Colour of coat is of importance in some breeds but not in

others. What coat colour is allowed in the following breeds?
a. Greyhound?
b. Nova Scotia Duck Tolling Retriever?
c. Curly Coated Retriever?

Section 6

The following questions are based on an individual's knowledge of breed standards. Each question is made up of 3 parts, each part consists of an extract from a breed standard. If the breed can be identified after 1 extract, a maximum of 3 points are awarded. If the breed is identified after 2 extracts, 2 points are awarded, etc.

400. a. <u>General appearance</u>
Agile, active watchdog and hunter of vermin. In appearance he is a small, thickset, black, tail-less dog, with a fox-like face. The dog is square in profile and possesses a distinctive coat, which includes a stand-out ruff, cape and culottes. All of these create a unique silhouette, appearing to slope from shoulders to croup . . .
b. <u>Size, proportion, substance</u>
The suggested height at the highest point of the withers is 11-13 inches for the male and 10-12 inches for bitches. . .
c. <u>Gait</u>
Proper – movement is smooth, well-coordinated and graceful trot (basically double tracking at a moderate speed) with a tendency to gradually converge towards the centre of balance beneath the dog as speed increases. . .

401. a. <u>General appearance</u>
Has the appearance of an active, intelligent, muscular dog of heavy bone, smooth coat, compactly built, and of medium or small structure. Expression alert, curious, and interested . . .
b. <u>Size, proportion, substance</u>
Weight not to exceed 28 pounds; over 28 pounds is a disqualification. Proportion - distance from withers to

ground in good relation to distance from withers to onset to the tail . . .

c. <u>Head</u>

Large and square. Eyes dark in colour, wide apart, set low in the skull, as far from the ears as possible, round in form, of moderate size, neither sunken nor bulging . . . Ears – known as bat ears, broad at the base, elongated with, round top, set high on the head but not too close together, and carried erect with the orifice to the front. . . Nose black . . . Flews black, thick and broad, hanging over the lower jaw at the sides, meeting the underlip in front and covering the teeth which are not seen when the mouth is closed. The underjaw is deep, square, broad, undershot and well turned up.

402. a. <u>General appearance</u>

Blue and tan coat is parted on the face and from the base of the skull to the end of the tail and hangs evenly and quite straight down each side of the body. The body is neat, compact and well proportioned. The dog's high head carriage and confident manner should give the appearance of vigour and self-importance.

b. <u>Tail</u>

Docked to medium length and carried slightly higher than the level of the back.

c. <u>Weight</u>

Must not exceed seven pounds.

403. a. <u>General appearance</u>

Game and hardy, with expressive dropped ears, is one of the smallest of the working terriers. It is active and compact, free-moving, with good substance and bone. With its natural, weather-resistant coat and short legs, it is a "perfect demon" in the field. This versatile, agreeable breed can go to ground, bolt a fox and tackle or dispatch other small vermin, working alone or with a pack. Honourable scars from wear and tear are acceptable in the ring.

b. <u>Size, proportion, substance</u>

Height at withers 9 to 10 inches at maturity . . . Length of back from point of the withers to base of the tail should be slightly longer than the height at the withers. . . Weight 11 to 12 pounds or that which is suitable for each individual dog's structure and balance. Fit working condition is a prime consideration.

c. <u>Colour</u>
All shades of red, wheaten, black and tan, or grizzle. Dark points permissible. White markings are not desirable.

404. a. <u>General appearance</u>
A graceful, alert, swift-moving little dog with saucy expression, compact, and with terrier-like qualities of temperament.
b. <u>Size, proportion, substance</u>
Weight – a well balanced dog not to exceed 6 pounds. Proportion – The body is off-square; hence, slightly longer when measured from point of shoulders to point of buttocks, than height at the withers. . .
c. <u>Head</u>
A well-rounded "apple-dome" skull with or without molera. Expression – Saucy. Eyes – Full, but not protruding, balanced, set well apart – luminous dark or luminous ruby. (Light eyes in blond or white-coloured dogs permissible). Ears – large, erect type, held more upright when alert, but flaring to the sides at a 45 degree angle when in repose, giving breath between the ears. Muzzle – moderately short, slightly pointed. Cheek and jaws lean. . . Bite – Level or scissors. . .

405. a. <u>General appearance</u>
A toy dog, fine-boned, elegant and graceful. The distinct varieties are born in the same litter . . .
b. <u>Bite</u>
Scissors or level in both varieties. missing teeth in the _____ are to be faulted. The _____ variety is not to be penalized for absence of full dentition.
c. <u>Coat</u>
The _____ variety has hair on certain portions of the

body: the head (called a crest), the tail (called a plume) and the feet from the toes to the front pasterns and rear hock joints (called stocks). The texture of all hair is soft and silky, flowing to any length. . . Wherever the body is hairless, the skin is soft and smooth. . . The _____ variety is completely covered with a double soft and silky coat . . .

406. a. <u>General appearance</u>
A graceful, lithe, well-balanced dog with no sign of coarseness, weakness or shelliness. In repose the expression is mild and gentle, not shy or nervous. Aroused, the dog is particularly alert and full of immense energy and courage. Noteworthy for endurance, _____ also gallop at great speed, as their body outline clearly shows.

b. <u>Head</u>
Narrow, but deep and rounded. Shorter in the skull and longer in the jaw. Covered in a profuse topknot which is lighter than the colour of the body, highest at the crown, and tapering gradually to just back of the nose. There must be no stop and the unbroken line from crown to nose end reveals a slender head without cheekiness or snipiness . . .
Ears - Triangular with rounded tips. Set on low and hanging flat to the cheek in front with a slight projection at the base. Thin and velvety in texture, covered with fine hair forming a small silky tassel at the tip. . .

c. <u>Body</u>
Muscular and markedly flexible. Chest deep. Flat-ribbed and deep through the brisket, which reaches the elbows. Back has a natural arch over the loin, creating a definite tuck-up of the underline. Body slightly greater in length than height. . .

407. a. <u>General appearance</u>
A small, black, short-coated dog with distinctive rich mahogany markings and a taper style tail. In structure the _____ presents a sleek, sturdy, yet elegant look, and has a wedge-shaped, long and clean head with a keen, bright, alert expression. . .

b. <u>Size</u>
The Toy variety shall not exceed 12 pounds . . . The Standard variety shall be over 12 pounds and not exceeding 22 pounds. . .
c. <u>Gait</u>
The gait should be free and effortless with good reach of the forequarters, showing no indication of hackney gait. . .

408. a. <u>General appearance</u>
A powerful, sturdy, squarely built, upstanding dog of Arctic type, medium in size with strong muscular development and heavy bone. The body is compact, short-coupled, broad and deep, tail set high and carried closely to the back, the whole supported by four straight, strong, sound legs. . . The large head with broad, flat skull and short, broad and deep muzzle is proudly carried and accentuated by a ruff. . .
b. <u>Coat</u>
There are two types of coat; rough and smooth. Both are double coated. In the rough coat, the outer coat is abundant, dense, straight and offstanding, rather coarse in texture; the undercoat soft, thick and woolly. . . The coat forms a profuse ruff around the head and neck, framing the head . . .
c. <u>Gait</u>
Proper movement is the crucial test of proper conformation and soundness. It must be sound, straight moving, agile, brieg, quick, and powerful, never lumbering. The rear gait short and stilted because of the straighter rear assembly. It is from the side that the unique stilted action is most easily assessed.

409. a. <u>General appearance</u>
A natural, handsome dog of well-balanced, short-coupled body, attracting attention not only by his coloration, alert carriage, and intelligent expression, but also by his stand-off coat, his richly plumed tail well curled over his back, his foxlike expression, and his small pointed ears. His coat is thick around the neck, fore part of the shoulder and chest, forming a lion-like ruff – more profuse in the male. His rump and hind legs, down to the hocks, are also thickly coated, forming the characteristic "trousers". His head, ears,

and lower legs are covered with thick, short hair.

b. Head

Expression is largely dependent on the distinctive characteristic called "spectacles" – a combination of marking and shading in the orbital area which must include a delicate, dark line slanting from the outer corner of each eye toward the lower corner of each ear coupled with expressive eyebrows . . .

c. Colour and markings

A dramatically marked dog, the _____ is a mixture of gray, black and cream. This coloration may vary from light to dark. The hair of the outer coat is black tipped, the length of the black tips producing the characteristic shading of colour. . .

410. a. General appearance

Lithe, strong, responsive, active dog, carrying no useless timber, standing naturally straight and firm. The deep, moderately wide chest shows strength, the sloping shoulders and well-bent hocks indicate speed and grace, and the face shows high intelligence. The _____ presents an impressive, proud picture of true balance, each part being in harmonious proportion to every other part and to the whole . . .

b. Coat

The well-fitting, proper-textured coat is the crowning glory of the rough variety.   It is abundant except on the head and legs. The outercoat is straight and harsh to the touch. A soft, open outer coat or a curly outer coat, regardless of quantity is penalized. . . The texture, quantity and the extent to which the coat "fits the dog" are important points.

c. Colour

The four recognised colors are "Sable and White", "tri-color", "Blue Merle" and "White". There is no preference among them . . .

411. a. Size, proportion, substance

Should be "multum in parvo", and this condensation (if the word may be used) is shown by compactness in form, well knit proportions, and hardness of developed muscle. Weight from 14 to 18 pounds (dog or bitch) desirable. Proportion square.

b. Head

The head is massive, round – not apple-headed, with no indentation of the skull. The eyes are dark in colour, very large, bold and prominent, globular in shape, soft and solicitous in expression, very lustrous, and when excited full of fire. The ears are thin, small, soft, like black velvet. There are two kinds – the "rose" and the "button". Preference is given to the latter. The wrinkles are large and deep. The muzzle is short, blunt, square, but not upfaced. . .

c. Markings

The markings are clearly defined. The muzzle, or mask, ears, mole on cheeks, thumb mark or diamond on forehead, and the back trace should be as black as possible. The mask should be black. The more intense and well defined it is, the better. The trace is a black line extending from the occiput to the tail.

412. a. General appearance

A dog of style, elegance and dignity: agile and strong with sturdy bone and hard muscle. Long, low and level – he is twice as long as he is high – he is covered with a profuse coat that falls straight down either side of the body over oval-shaped ribs. The hair well feathered on the head veils forehead and eyes to serve as protection from brush and briar as well as amid serious encounters with other animals. He stands with head high and long tail hanging and moves with a seemingly effortless gait. He is strong in body, quarters and jaw.

b. Size, proportion, substance

The ideal shoulder height for dogs is 10 inches and bitches 9.5 inches. . . The ideal ration of body length to shoulder height is 2 to 1, which is considered the correct proportion. .

c. Colour

The coat must be of one over-all colour at the skin but may be of varying shades of the same color in the full coat, which may be black, blue, dark or light grey, silver platinum, fawn or cream. The dog must have no distinctive markings except for desirable black points of ears, muzzle and tip of tail, all of which points are preferably dark even black. The shade of head and legs should approximate that of the body. There must be no trace of pattern, design or clear-cut colour deviation, with the exception of the breed's only permissible white which occasionally exists on the chest not exceeding 2 inches in diameter. The puppy coat may be very different in colour from the adult coat. . .

413. a. General

Powerful, proportionately tall figure, strong and muscular in every part, with powerful head and most intelligent expression. In dogs with a dark mask the expression appears more stern, but never ill-natured.

b. Colour

White with red or red with white, the red in its various shades; brindle patches with white markings. The colours red and brown-yellow are of entirely equal value. Necessary markings are: white chest, feet and tip of tail, noseband, collar or spot on the nape; the latter and blaze are very desirable. Never of one colour or without white. Faulty are all other colours, except the favourite dark shadings on the head (mask) and ears. One distinguishes between mantle and splash-coated dogs.

c. Height at shoulder

Of the dog should be 27.5 inches minimum, of the bitches 25 inches. Female animals are of finer and more delicate build.

414. a. General appearance

A toy dog, intelligent, alert, sturdy, with a thickset, short body, a smart carriage and set-up, attracting attention by an almost human expression. There are two distinct types of coat: rough or smooth. Except for the coat, there is no difference between the two.

b. Head

An almost human expression. Eyes set well apart, very large, black, prominent, and well open. The eyelashes long and black. Eyelids edged with black. Ears small and set rather high on the head. . . carried semi-erect. Skull large and round, with a domed forehead. The stop deep. Nose very black, extremely short, its tip being set back deeply betwen the eyes so as to form a lay-back. The nostrils large . . .

c. Colour

Either 1) Red: reddish brown with a little black at the whiskers and chin allowable; 2) Beige: black and reddish brown mixed, usually with black mask and whiskers; 3) Black and tan: black with uniform reddish brown markings, appearing under the chin, on the legs, above each eye, around the edges of the ears and around the vent; or 4) Black: solid black. Any white hairs are a serious fault, except for "frost" on the muzzle of a mature dog, which is natural . Disqualification – white spot or blaze anywhere on coat.

415. a. General appearance

An aristocrat, his whole appearance of dignity and aloofness with no trace of plainness or coarseness. He has a straight front, proudly carried head, eyes gazing into the distance, as if in memory of ages past. The striking characteristics of the breed – exotic, or "Eastern" expression, long silky top-knot, peculiar coat pattern, very prominent hipbones, large feet, and the impression of a somewhat exaggerated bend in the stifle due to profuse trousering – stand out clearly, giving the _____ the appearance of what he is, a king of dogs, that has held true to tradition throughout the ages.

b. Coat

Hindquarters, flank, ribs, forequarters, and legs well covered with thick, silky hair, very fine in texture, ears and all four feet well feathered; from in front of the shoulders; and also backwards from the shoulders along the saddle from the flanks and the ribs upwards, the hair is short and close, forming a smooth back in mature dogs . . .

c. Gait

When running free, moves at a gallop, showing great elasticity and spring in his smooth, powerful stride. When on a loose lead, can trot at a fast pace; stepping along, he has the appearance of placing the hind feet directly in the foot prints of the front feet, both thrown straight ahead. . .

416. a.   Size, proportion, substance

The height of the _____ as measured at the withers ranges from 13 to 15 inches. Any deviation from these measurements is a minor fault. The weight ranges between 35 and 45 pounds. Proportion - The _____ presents a rectangular outline as the breed is longer in body tha it is tall. Substance – The _____ is muscular and rather massive.

b.   Head

Correct head and expression are important features of the breed. The eyes are hazel in colour, fairly large, soft and languishing, but do not show the haw overmuch. Has a sombre and serious appearance, and its heavy brows produce a frowning expression. The ears are thick, fairly large, and lobe-shaped and are set moderately low, slightly, above the outside corner of the eye. The skull is moderately long and also wide with an indentation in the middle and with a full stop. . . The muzzle should be approximately three inches long, broad, and square in profile. The skull as measured from the stop to the occiput is longer than the muzzle. The nostrils are well developed and liver colored. The lips are somewhat pendulous. . .

c.   Colour

Rich golden liver is the only acceptable colour and is a certain sign of the purity of the breed. Dark liver or puce is a major fault. White on the chest is a minor fault. White on any other part of the body is a major fault.

417. a.   General appearance

The whole appearance of this breed should give an impression of grace and symmetry and of great speed and endurance coupled with strength and activity to enable it to kill gazelle or other quarry over deep sand or rocky mountains. The expression should be dignified and gentle with deep, faithful, far-seeing eyes. Dogs should average in height from 23 to 28 inches and bitches may be considerably smaller, this being very typical of the breed.

b.   Head

Long and narrow, skull moderately wide between the ears, not domed, stop not pronounced, the whole showing great quality. Nose black or liver. Ears long and covered with long silky hair hanging close to the skull and mobile. Eyes dark to hazel and bright; large and oval, but not prominent. teeth strong and level.

c. Colour

White, cream, fawn, golden, red, grizzle and tan, tricolor (white, black and tan) and black and tan.

418. a. General appearance

Medium-sized dog, profusely coated, of powerful build, and square in proportion. A fall of hair covers the eyes and foreface. The well-feathered tail curls up and falls forward over the back. The feet are large, flat, and round in shape producing a snowshoe effect that provides traction. The _____ is well balanced and capable of both strong and efficient movement. The _____ is shown as naturally as possible.

b. Neck, topline, body

Neck – length proportionate to the body and head. Body – compact, square and strong, capable of both speed and endurance. Topline – the back is level in motion. Chest – Heavily furnished. The brisket extends downward to the top of the elbow in the mature _____. Ribs – The body is well ribbed up and never cloddy or coarse. The rib cage is not too wide across the chest and narrows slightly to permit the forelegs to work freely at the sides . . .

c. Coat

Double coat. Undercoat is soft and woolly. Outer coat is profuse and fine but never silky or woolly. May be wavy or straight. Coat is long but should not hang to the ground. When standing on a hard surface an area of light should be seen under the dog. The coat of puppies is shorter, single and often has a softer texture than that of adults. . .

419. a. General appearance

Possesses, in a most marked degree, every point and characteristic of those dogs which hunt together by scent (Sagaces). He is very powerful, and stands over more ground than is usual with hounds of other breeds. The skin is thin to the touch and extremely loose, this being more especially noticeable about the head and neck, where it hangs in deep folds.

b. Weight

The mean average weight of adult dogs, in fair condition, is 90 pounds, and of adult bitches 80 pounds. Dogs attain the weight of 110 pounds, bitches 100 pounds. The greater weights are to be preferred, provided (as in the case of Height) that quality and proportion are also combined.

c. Head

The head is narrow in proportion to its length, and long in proportion to the body, tapering but slightly from the temples to the end of the muzzle, thus (when viewed from above and in front) having the appearance of being flattened at the sides and of being nearly equal in width throughout its entire length. . . The skull is long and narrow, with the occipital peak very pronounced. . .The eyes are deeply sunk in the orbits, the lids assuming a lozenge or diamond shape, in consequence of the lower lids being dragged down and everted by the heavy flews. The eyes correspond with the general tone of the animal, varying from deep hazel to yellow . . . The head is furnished with an amount of loose skin, which in nearly every position appears superabundant, but more particularly so when the head is carried low . . . In the front the lips fall squarely, making a right angle with the upper line of the foreface, whilst behind they form deep, hanging flews, and being continued into the pendant folds of loose skin about the neck, constitute the dewlap, which is very pronounced . . .

420. a. General appearance

Bred primarily for sport field; he should unmistakably look and act the part. The ideal specimen gives the immediate impression of compact power and agile grace; the head noble, proudly carried; the expression intelligent and alert; the muscular body bespeaking both staying power and dash. Here is an animal whose every movement shows him to be a wide-a-wake, hard driving hunting dog possessing stamina, courage, and the desire to go. . .

b. Head

The skull of medium width, approximately as wide as the
length of the muzzle, resulting in an impression of length
rather than width. Slight furrow between the eyes, cheeks
cleanly chiselled. There should be a pronounced stop.
Parallel planes of the skull and muzzle are equally
acceptable. The muzzle should be deep without pendulous
flews. Jaws ending square and level, should bite evenly or
as scissors. Nostrils well developed and wide open. Ears
set on at eye level. When hanging naturally, they should
reach just below the lower jaw, close to the head, with little
or no folding. . . Eye – of ample size, rounded and intense.
The eye colour should be dark in contrast with the colour of
the markings, the darker the better.

c. Colour

Liver, lemon, black, orange; either in combination with
white or solid-coloured . . .

421. a. General appearance

A toy dog covered from head to foot with a mantle of long,
silky, white hair. He is gentle-mannered and affectionate,
eager and sprightly in action, and despite his size, possessed
of the vigour needed for the satisfactory companion.

b. Coat and colour

The coat is single, that is, without undercoat. It hangs long,
flat, and silky over the sides of the body almost, if not quite,
to the ground. The long head-hair may be tied up in a
topknot or it may be left hanging. Any suggestion of
kinkiness, curliness, or woolly texture is objectionable.
Colour, pure white. Light tan or lemon on the ears is
permissible, but not desirable.

c. Gait

Moves with a jaunty, smooth, flowing gait. Viewed from
the side, he gives an impression of rapid movement, size
considered. In the stride, the forelegs reach straight and free
from the shoulders, with elbows close. Hind legs to move in
a straight line. Cowhocks or any suggestion of hind leg
toeing in or out are faults.

422. a. <u>Head</u>

Long and narrow, fairly wide between the ears, scarcely perceptible stop, little or no development of nasal sinuses, good length of muzzle, which should be powerful without coarseness. Teeth very strong and even in front. Ears small and fine in texture, thrown back and folded, except when excited, when they are semipricked. Eyes – dark, bright, intelligent, indicating spirit.

b. <u>Hindquarters</u>

Long, very muscular and powerful, wide and well let-down, well-bent stifles. Hocks well bent and rather low to ground, wide but straight fore and aft.

c. <u>Weight</u>

Dogs, 65 to 70 pounds; bitches, 60 to 65 pounds.

423. a. <u>Head</u>

Long and well proportioned, skull not too flat, jaws long and strong but not inclined to snipiness, nose black, in the black coated variety, with wide nostrils. Teeth strong and level. Eyes black or brown, but not yellow, rather large but not too prominent. Ears rather small, set on low, lying close to the head, and covered with short curls.

b. <u>Coat</u>

Should be one mass of crisp curls all over. A slightly more open coat not to be severly penalised, but a saddle back or patch of uncurled hair behind the shoulder should be penalised, and a prominent white patch on breast is undesirable, but a few white hairs allowed in an otherwise good dog. Colour, black or liver.

c. <u>Tail</u>

Should be moderately short, carried fairly straight and covered with curls, slightly tapering towards the point.

424. a. <u>Skull</u>

Massive, broad, wide and flat between the ears (not dome-shaped), wide between the eyes. Nose – black, broad, very short and flat. Eyes – Large, dark, prominent, round, lustruous. Stop – Deep. Ears – Heart-shaped, not set too high, leathers never long enough to come below the muzzle,

nor carried erect but drooping, long feather. Muzzle –
Wrinkled, very short and broad, not overshot nor pointed.
Strong, broad underjaw, teeth not to show.

b.   Shape of body

Heavy in front, well-sprung ribs, broad chest, falling away
lighter behind, lionlike. Back level. Not too long in body;
allowance made for longer body in bitch. Legs – Short
forelegs, bones of forearm bowed, firm at shoulder; hind
legs lighter but firm and well shaped. Feet – Flat, toes
turned out, not round, should stand well up on feet, not on
ankles.

Chapter 3

Veterinary, health and anatomy questions

425. What is meant by describing a dog as "sound"?
426. What is meant by "type"?
427. What is a dog's conformation?
428. What is angulation?
429. What is a "well-turned" dog?
430. Canine breed standards draw upon many descriptive terms and phrases used originally to describe what other animal?
431. What is a dog's topline?
432. How many bones are there in a dog's body? Approx 210, 320 or 450 bones?
433. What is the largest organ of the dog's body?
434. How many pairs of ribs does a dog have?
435. How many toes or digits (excluding dewclaws) does a dog have?
436. How many bones or phalanges are there in each toe?
437. Water accounts for what percentage of a dog's weight? Is it approx 40, 50 or 70%?
438. What is the largest single bone in a dog's body?
439. Which is the longest tendon in a dog's body?
440. Which is the dog's floating rib?
441. What is the common name for the brisket?
442. What is the stifle joint in the rear leg commonly known as?
443. How many pads are on the sole of a dog's foot?
444. Dogs have an additional pad located at the back of the wrists (carpus) on the forelegs. What is it called, and what does it do?
445. Fractures, dislocations and sprains are the result of injuries to which part of the body?
446. What is the normal temperature of a dog?
447. Is the normal temperature of puppy the same as an adult dog?
448. What is the average cardiac rhythm of a dog?
449. The brain of a St Bernard weighs approximately 15% of that

of a human brain. True or false?

450. A dog should have 42 teeth. How many on the top and how many on the bottom?

451. How many milk or temporary teeth does a puppy have?

452. What is inbreeding?

453. A puppy is born blind, deaf and cannot smell. What sensory mechanism doe s it rely on for the first 2 weeks of its life?

454. Sometimes a bitch after she has given birth can develop eclampsia. What causes this condition?

455. Who was the founder of genetics?

456. What do the initials A.I. stand for?

457. Is the father (sire) or the mother (dam) responsible for the sex of the puppies?

458. How long does a bitch's pregnancy last?

459. How many teats does a bitch have normally?

460. What does the genetic profile of a dog determine?

461. What is a congenital defect?

462. What is an "entire" dog?

463. What is meant by the term "desexing" a dog?

464. What is P.R.A.?

465. Which part of the body does P.R.A. affect?

466. Canine distemper is a highly contagious viral disease. By what other name is it known by and why?

467. Otitis externa or canker is an infection associated with which part of a dog's body?

468. Is rabies a viral or bacterial disease?

469. Dogs are susceptable to Lyme Disease. What parasite is most widely associated with it?

470. When would you use an Elizabethan collar on a dog?

471. Where would you feel to obtain an accurate reading of a dog's pulse?

472. Do dogs dream?

473. Why should you clean your dog's teeth?

474. What are the 5 basic nutritional ingredients required by a dog?

475. Why should a dog's bed be raised off the ground?

476. Bones have little or no nutritional value, but are important for aiding digestion, and are indispensible for what other reason?

477. What type of bones should never be given to dogs?
478. What is meant by the term "canine olfaction"?
479. Name 2 methods for stopping a dog from bleeding.
480. A dog's sense of smell and hearing are more highly developed than its eyesight. True or false?
481. Does a dog have ultrasonic hearing?
482. Hip Dysplasia is a disease affecting a dog's hindquarters. What is it?
483. When a dog's hackles rise, what happens and why?
484. When cutting a dog's nails, what should you avoid?
485. What is meant by describing a dog as having "hard flesh"?
486. If a dog is described as "bossy", what is it?
487. What are a dog's fetlocks more commonly known as?
488. Which highly contagious viral disease first appeared in 1978, the symptoms of which are similar to those of infectious feline enteritis?
489. When running, a dog's body must stay parallel with the ground. True or false?
490. When a dog moves from trotting to gallop, does he increase the frequency of stride, or increase the length of stride?
491. Which breeds or group of dogs have a double-suspension gallop, which was needed to match that of the prey they originally pursued?
492. Which breed of dog is the fastest?
493. How many vertebrae bones are there in a dog's back (thoracic or lumbar regions)?
494. How do dogs perspire?
495. What are dewclaws?
496. Why should you groom a dog?
497. What type of coat is never brushed?
498. Some dogs have a double coat. What type of coat is it?
499. Certain breeds, such as the Irish Water Spaniel and the Curly Coated Retriever have a curly coat. What is the specialised function of this type of coat?
500. Kennel Cough is a highly contagious disease, also known as viral tracheitis. Most dogs become infected in places where numbers of dogs congregate. How is it transmitted?
501. What is the function of the pasterns, and where are they located?

502. In mating, what is the "tie"?
503. What is colostrum?
504. What is a dudley nose?
505. What is the flap of a dog's ear called?
506. What is the stop?
507. If a dog is wall-eyed, what does it have?
508. What is a full eye?
509. If a dog has paper thin feet, what does it have?
510. What are pin toes?
511. What are snowshoe feet?
512. Anatomically, the cheetah is intermediate between the cat and the dog. True or false?
513. The wolf howls, and in general dogs bark. Name a breed of dog that howls.
514. A dog's diet requires essential vitamins and minerals. What results from a deficiency of the following:
    a Vitamin D.
    b Vitamin B12
515. Which is a dog's lumbar area?

Chapter 4

Rules and Regulations Questions

Section 1 – US

516. How many groups of breeds are recognised by the American Kennel Club?
517. What is an American-bred dog?
518. How long does a person have to register a litter with the AKC?
519. Can an individual puppy from a litter be registered with the AKC?
520. The AKC will normally only register a litter born to a dam, which meets its age restrictions. What are the limitations?
521. The AKC will normally only register a litter sired by a dog which meets its age restrictions. What are the limitations?
522. Can you change the name of a dog registered with the AKC?
523. What is the usual length of time a registered prefix is granted for?
524. The protection of kennel names registered between March 1, 1934 and October 1, 1948 depends on the registered owners doing what?
525. Can a puppy born to a dog with limited registration be registered?
526. In considering the registration of a new breed, the AKC must consider whether the breed has been in existence long enough to be considered a separate pure breed. What other 2 considerations must also be considered?
527. Will the AKC consider an individual's application to register a new breed?
528. Does the AKC register litters whelped outside the US?
529. What is the AKC's Miscellaneous Class?
530. How long does a new breed spend in the Miscellaneous Class?

531. What activities can a breed in the Miscellaneous Class compete in?

532. For how long does the AKC require a dog's AKC record papers to be kept?

533. The AKC litter application – "The records of a litter produced by" form – requires that information regarding number of puppies whelped be described by sex, and what other 2 categories?

534. Which AKC department deals with record-keeping, identification practices, and investigates registration rule violations?

535. AKC registrations are dealt by the Registrations Department located in Raleigh, North Carolina. Does this department deal with the following special categories of registration? Foreign registrations, Coonhound registrations, limited registrations

536. What is a Member Show?

537. What is a Licensed Show?

538. What is a Group Show?

539. What is a Specialty show?

540. What is an American-bred Specialty show?

541. What is a Sanctioned match?

542. How many show or field trials can a club or association hold each year?

543. When may a Member club or association lose its sole show privilege?

544. What is the minimum age for a dog to be exhibited at a dog show, and are there any exceptions?

545. Puppy classes and Twelve-to-Eighteen Month classes are for dogs restricted by age, and excluding . . . ?

546. What is the Novice Class?

547. What is an Open Class?

548. What is the Winners Class?

549. Is there an entry fee for competition in the Winners Class?

550. A Club that provides Winners Classes must also provide what other competitions?

551. How many points does a dog need to win to become a Champion of Record?

552. How many points can a dog gain at any one show?

553. What determines how many points will be awarded in classes at different shows?
554. Number of points are not the only requirement for Champion status. What other qualifications are required?
555. When must a dog earn 3 "legs"?
556. What are the 3 levels of Obedience Trials?
557. What are Tracking Tests?
558. What do the initials TDX stand for when used in connection with Tracking Tests?
559. Does the AKC authorise field trials for Basset Hounds and Dachshunds?
560. What is a "Master Hunter" title?
561. The AKC Herding Program is divided into 2 sections. Can you name them?
562. What does the Herding Test Dog (HT) title signify?
563. What does the Pre-Trial Tested Dog (PT) title signify?
564. How many points are required to gain the Herding Championship (HCH)?

Section 2 – FCI

565. What are the 2 types of FCI membership?
566. Only one national organization from each country may be accepted by the FCI. Can you state which type of membership do the following countries hold?
a. France
b. Spain
c. Bahrain
d. Ireland
e. Great Britain
f. United States
g. Australia
h. Japan

567. The General Assembly of the FCI is formed by the full membership, and meets at least once every two years. How many delegates does each full member send to the Assembly?
568. The General Committee carries out the decisions of the

General Assembly, and consists of 6 members from different full members. Members are elected and serve what period of time in office?

569. How often does the General Committee meet?

570. Each canine society which becomes a member of the FCI is assigned to one of the 5 regional groups. Can you name 3?

571. Which officers form the Executive Committee, which carry out the decisions of the General Committee of the FCI?

572. The FCI has 3 compulsory commissions. Can you name 1?

573. What are the 4 official languages of the FCI?

574. What must each governing national organisation provide the FCI with regards to their own breed standards?

575. Who is responsible for the approval of a new breed standard?

576. Who must be consulted before a new standard or modification to existing standard can be accepted?

577. When a new or modified standard is approved, how is it published?

578. Do members of the FCI recognise each other's stud books, pedigrees, and kennel names?

579. Does the FCI maintain an international register of kennel names?

580. Can a kennel name registered by a national authority be cancelled if it causes damage to a kennel name registered by the FCI?

581. What type of events are held under the patronage of the FCI?

582. Who is responsible for the training, examining and listing of judges?

583. Each national governing organisation must produce an annual judges list which is circulated to all members. What information must it contain?

584. How many breed groups does the FCI recognise?

585. What do the intitals CACIB stand for?

586. What must shows at which CACIBs are awarded be advertised as?

587. How many CACIBs are granted to member organisations per year?

588. How many CACIBs can be awarded at one show?

589. The CACIB can be awarded in 3 classes. Can you name 1?
590. What qualification (1 of 2) must a dog have if entered into the Championship Class?
591. What minimum age is required for competing for CACIBs?
592. Judges at a FCI show with CACIBs must award titles in accordance to 4 definitions, ranging from Excellent to Fairly Good. What is the definition of Excellent?
593. What is the definition of Fairly Good?
594. Once a year, the FCI hold a World Dog Show at which the title Winner of the World Show is awarded for all breeds recognised by the FCI. Entry for which classes qualify?
595. Is there a Reserve Winner of the World Show?
596. Can an international judge from a country not affiliated to the FCI judge an FCI show?
597. How many CACIBs are required to qualify for the title International Beauty Champion if not a breed subject to working trials?
598. What is the minimum age for an FCI International Dog Show judge?
599. A candidate who wishes to be approved as a judge must pass a written examination, and undergo a series of practical tests. What must the practical test be based on?
600. The FCI recognises 3 types of judges. Can you name them?
601. What is the maximum number of dogs that a FCI judge can handle if an individual report on each dog is required by the national organisation?
602. What is the maximum number of dogs an FCI judge can handle if no individual reports on the dogs are required?
603. Which annual FCI event is the "summit meeting" of Agility competitors, and the winner is awarded the title "Agility European Winner"?
604. How many dogs can each FCI member organisation select to compete in the annual Agility competition?
605. What is an agility dog's working book, and is it compulsory for FCI competitions?
606. In which competitions would Natural Qualities Certificates (NQC) be issued?
607. What decision was taken at the 1976 Innsbruck Meeting regarding field trials?

608. Which FCI Field Trials are regarded as "Trials in the English fashion"?
609. The Spring European Cup for Continental Pointers is run solely on what game?
610. How many dogs can be included in the national teams competing in the Spring European Cup for Continental Pointers?
611. The FCI has working trial competitions (RIC) which are divided into 2 sections. Can you name them?
612. How many RCI grades are there in an international FCI competition?
613. RIC working trial competitions are marked on a point system, with a maximum of 300 points. What distinction would be obtained with a final score of 100?

Section 3 – Australia

614. Australian dog shows are divided into 3 types of dog shows, and several categories of competitions. What are the 3 types of show?
615. Can an Australian Champion dog compete in an Open Show?
616. What is an Open Parade?
617. At which show are Challenge Certificate points awarded, which are counted towards the title of Champion?
618. What is a Sanctioned Competition?
619. Australian dog shows are divided into 11 different classes. What is Baby Puppy class?
620. What is the Intermediate Class?
621. What is the Novice Class?
622. What is a State-Bred Class?
623. What is an Australian Bred Class?
624. What is an Open Class?
625. How many breed groups are recognised by the Australian National Kennel Control?
626. How many classes are there in Obedience Trials
627. If a dog has won a variety of Obedience titles can all of them be used after his name?

628. If a dog has competed in an Open Obedience Class can it compete in a Novice Class?
629. What class title do the initials CDX signify?
630. How many dogs must compete in Obedience Group Exercises?
631. If a dog has received a non-qualifying score will it automatically be removed from the competition?
632. If the Obedience Ring is to be used for a multiple of classes, including Utility Dog and Novice Classes, which class must be judged first?
633. All dogs in Obedience competitions usually wear collars. What is the minimum length of lead required?
634. All exercises in Novice, Open and Utility classes are executed off-lead, with the exception of which 2 exercises?
635. Does the dog enter or leave the ring on a lead?
636. The food provided for the Food Refusal Exercise in Obedience competition must be of how many different varieties?
637. When would over 50% of the marks be deducted from an Heel on Lead Obedience Trial score?
638. What is the maximum number of points which can be scored at an Obedience Trial?
639. What qualifications must a dog have to compete in Tracking Trials?
640. What tests must a dog pass to obtain a Tracking Dog (TD) title?
641. What is a tracklayer?
642. What is the minimum age for a dog to compete in Agility Trials?
643. What is the minimum number of dogs and handlers required for an Agility Trial?
644. The title Agility Dog (AD) requires a dog to have gained a qualification card at how many Agility Trials?
645. What is required to gain a Qualification card at an Agility Trial?
646. What is the height limit, which will determine whether a dog competes in the small dog section, or the large dog section of an Agility Trial?

647. What is the maximum number of dogs which can be judged by one judge in an Agility Trial held in connection with an Obedience Trial?

648. Is there a time limit for completion of the 1st round of an Agility Test?

649. If a dog achieves a clear round in an Agility Trial, what does it receive?

650. How many penalty seconds are added to the Agility course time for each mistake or fault made during to a round?

651. Prior to the start of each Agility Trial what must the judge ask the handler?

652. All Agility judging finishes when the judge orders "Test finished", except in which instance?

653. Name a breed which competes in Utility Gundog Field Trials?

654. Do Non-Slip Retrieving Trials test dogs work on land and in, or through, water?

655. What is the function of a Non-Slip Retriever?

656. How many points are required to gain the title of Australian Retrieving Trial Champion?

657. What type of game is preferred for Utility Trials?

658. What is the minimum number of dogs required to hold a Stake at any Field Trial?

659. Do Special Stakes held at Utility Trials count towards Championship status?

660. How many Championship Field Trial Stakes for Utility Gundogs are held each year?

661. When may a Pointer or a Setter be awarded a qualifying certificate in a field trial?

662. What type of rise retrieve are Retrievers and Spaniels required to complete in Field Trials?

Section 4 – Britain

663. How many breed groups are recognised by The Kennel Club?

664. How many sporting groups?

665. What is the Kennel Club's Imported Register?

666. What type of dog is registered in the Obedience and Working Trials Register?

667. If a dog has qualified for entry to the Stud Book, can you change its name?

668. What is an Endorsement?

669. Can imported dogs be registered before they leave quarantine?

670. Can a dog be registered after it has been exported from Britain?

671. Can a dog with cropped ears take part in a Championship dog show?

672. A litter will not normally be registered if the dam has reached what age?

673. A litter will not normally be registered if the dam has already had how many litters?

674. Which group of pure-bred dogs are exempt from registration with the Kennel Club?

675. What do the initials CNAF signify?

676. Some breeds are registered by more than one organisation in Britain. Which organisation has the suffix MHBA, which is included in its Kennel CLub registration details?

677. There are 5 types of registered society. Can you name 3?

678. What are Affiliated organisations?

679. What is the Ringcraft register?

680. What is a Breed Council?

681. How many licensed shows can an Agricultural Society hold per year?

682. When must registered and affiliated clubs renew their maintenance of title?

683. How many types of Kennel Club licensed shows are there?

684. At which shows are Champions and Challenge Certificate winners not allowed to compete?

685. What is an Exemption Show?

686. What is a Sanction Show?

687. What is the minimum size of a show judging ring?

688. How many awards must be on offer in every show class?

689. What is the minimum age that a dog can be exhibited at a show?

690. Does a show society have to issue a show catalogue?

691. When must 8 breed classes, including Limit and Open, be scheduled if Challenge Certificates are available for a breed?

692. When do wins at Championship Shows only count as wins at Open Shows?

693. How many Irish Kennel Club show awards count towards gaining the title of Champion?

694. What is a Show Champion?

695. What is a Veteran?

696. How many dogs of one breed are required to make up a show team?

697. In which type of event would you find Pre-Beginner and Class A, B, & C competitions?

698. In what type of event would you find elementary, starters, seniors, and advanced classes?

699. In Agility, what is the dog walk?

700. What is the minimum age for a dog to compete in Working Trials?

701. What 2 stakes are held annually, and form the Kennel Club Working Trial Championships?

702. Do wins at members Working Trials count in Championship or Open Working Trials?

703. What is a Working Trial Rally?

704. In Bloodhound Trials, when is a dog considered to have made a satisfactory identification?

705. When may Bloodhounds be allowed to hunt free?

706. Name 2 of the 4 field trial sub-groups of gundogs?

707. What is a Junior Warrant?

708. What is the highest class that may be offered at a Sanction Show?

709. How many dogs can compete at an Agility Match Meeting?

710. What eliminates a dog in an Agility competition?

711. What is an Interim Breed Standard?

712. What is a Stud Book number?

Chapter 5

Shows and Showing Questions

Section 1

713. Which was the first organised dog show in the world?

714. The first British dog show was limited to 2 types of dog. Name both.

715. What was the total entry for the first British dog show? Was it 60, 100 or 150 dogs?

716. Which early British dog show was the first all-breed classification, dividing the breedings into sporting and non-sporting, the forerunner of the present group divisions?

717. Which was the first written stud record and chronological list of dog shows published in the US?

718. The 1st American dog competition was held on June 2nd 1874, Illinois State Sportsmen's Association of Chicago. Why was this not regarded as the first proper American dog show?

719. Which is regarded as the first American Dog Show?

720. Under whose rules was the first American dog show organised?

721. Which was the first Field Trial held in Britain?

722. Which was the first Field Trial held in the US?

723. When did the Westminster Kennel Club hold its first show?

724. Why did the first Westminster Club Dog Show have to be extended for an extra day?

725. Which American sporting event precedes the Westminster Show in terms of longevity?

726. Which is the longest running Championship dog show in GB?

727. What is the main show/competition for hunting hounds in GB?

728. Which was the first Hound Show in GB?

729. Which was the first Scottish dog show to be held?

730. When did the Kennel Club stop recognising shows unless licensed under their jurisdiction? Was it 1875, 1882, or 1910?

731. Which is the premier Australian dog show?

732. What were the Pot House Shows?

733. What were Ribbon Shows?

734. In America, which dog show is called "The Garden Show" and why?

735. Which British dog show is known as the "northern classic"?

736. Charles Cruft organised his first dog show in 1886, which was restricted to which breeds?

737. When did Cruft's Dog Show become an all-breeds show? Was it 1891, 1899, or 1901?

738. Cruft's Dog Shows were traditionally held in London, but recently moved to Birmingham. In which year was show transfered northwards?

739. Charles Cruft died in 1938 and his widow organised the 1939 show. Who bought the title to the show, and organised the 1948 show?

740. The Kennel Club held its own dog shows twice a year. Why did the Club stop?

741. At which British dog show was there a class (no. 220) which was for stuffed dogs, and dogs made of wood, china, marble, etc?

742. At which British dog show were Army and Navy classes held for dogs owned by officers, NCOs, and the men?

743. At which British dog show were dogs from at least 3 European royal families entered?

744. When did the Ladies' Kennel Association hold its first dog show? Was it 1875, 1885, or 1895?

745. At which Scottish dog show did King George V enter 2 Labradors who won the Challenge Certificate, Best Gundog, and Reserve Best in Show awards?

746. What were the "Ladies Championships" held in GB?

747. Which British dog show made cinema history when its children's costume classes were filmed for Pathe Gazette's first newsreel talkies?

748. Which Irish dog shows award Kennel Club Challenge Certificates?

749. Which was the American Kennel Club's 1st sponsored show and what did it commemorate?

750. In 1924, the AKC introduced new group divisions, and standardized competitions. Which was the first show to include the Best in Show award under the new format?

751. Who won Best in Show, at Westminster Dog Show, 1924?

752. In which year was the Best in Show award first offered at Crufts?

753. Who won the first Best in Show award at Crufts?

754. The American Kennel Club celebrated its centenary with a dog show, only one of 2 which the Club had ever directly produced. When and where was it held?

755. Who won Best in Show at the AKC's Centennial Show?

756. Who won Best in Show at the Cruft's Centenary Show?

757. Who judged Best in Show at the AKC's Centennial Show?

758. Who judged Best in Show at the Cruft's Centenary Show?

759. At which famous British dog show did a cast of 300 actors perform a "Theatrical celebration and special centenary pageant"?

760. When was the Australian Bicentennial Championship Show held?

761. Who organises the "St Patrick's Day Show" in Ireland?

762. Who was responsible for the organising the dog section of the Paris Exhibition of 1878?

763. For which dog show did the dog food manufacturer, Spratt's, bake a 2 ton biscuit, which was displayed at Crystal Palace?

764. When and where were the first Sheep Dog Trials held in GB?

765. Who won the first sheep dog trial held in Australia?

766. The Canberra Kennel and Trial Dog Association was formed in 1944, and for several years held their dog shows and sheep dog trials at Manuka Oval, and which other unusual venue?

767. At which Australian dog shows were Prince William and Prince Richard trophies awarded for puppy and junior sweepstakes competition, being presented by their father, the Duke of Gloucester, who was the Governor-General?

768. Which American breed club held a special Breed Specialty Show in the ballroom of the Waldorf Astoria Hotel, New York, in 1898?

769. WELKS is one of the first British Championship shows in the annual show calendar. What do the intials stand for?

770. The British Three Counties Championship Dog Show is held as part of the Three Counties Agricultural Society Show. Name the 3 counties?

771. The Cleveland Society annual show held in Yorkshire was a specialist show, which is closely linked with the development of which breed of dog?

772. At the Dublin dog show in 1874, there were classes for 2 types of Irish Terrier. How were the classes divided?

773. The first all-breeds dog show to be held in Britain was in Birmingham in 1860. Which was the only terrier to have its own class?

774. Which breed was first shown in Britain at the Richmond Championship Show in July 1932?

775. In February 1928, Time Magazine published an article reviewing a dog show from the point of view of a Basset puppy, which featured on the front cover. What was the show?

776. Which British canine society was revived to run dog shows to raise funds for the Animal Health Trust?

777. Which American dog show was the first to be broadcast on network TV?

778. When did Sunday dog shows first appear in GB?

779. In which year did the first British General Championship Show do without prize money?

780. Which was the first British Championship Show to be held on a public Bank holiday?

781. In 1939, Blackpool Championship Show was the first British 2-day show to break with an established show tradition. What did the Show do?

782. Birmingham Dog Show Society is only 1 of 4 which has representative status to its annual shows i.e. right to award Challenge Certificates for all breeds eligible for CCs. Name one of the other 3?

783. In which year was the Scottish Kennel Club allowed to grant licences for Scottish dog shows?

784. Why was Crufts cancelled in 1954?

785. Why was the Richmond Championship Dog Show cancelled

in 1967?

786. Name the 3 types of British Championship Show?

787. At which show would you find the Kennel Club Obedience Championships?

788. Where are the Astro World Series of dog Shows held in America?

789. When were closing dates for show entries (not less than 7 days before the show) introduced in GB? Was it 1900, 1947, or 1960?

790. Life-saving Trials were first organised in GB in 1929. Which breed competes?

791. When were Non-Slip Retrieving Trials introduced into Australia?

792. When were Utility Field Trials for pointing-retrieving breeds introduced into Australia?

793. What are the American Kennel Club National Bird Dog Championships?

794. Where were the 1992 Retriever Championships, organised and run by the International Gundog League, held?

795. At the first British Field Trial at Southill, which breed took the first 3 places?

796. French hounds are generally regarded as dual purpose, suitable for shows and work. What is the main French hound show?

797. The Speciale Venerie covers every French hound breed, divided into specific classes for single hounds, pairs, etc. Name one other group class?

798. The Association of Bloodhound Breeders, and the Bloodhound Club both run Bloodhound Trials in GB. How many trials do each Club hold per year?

799. How many sheep dog trials does the International Sheep Dog Society hold each year in GB? Is it 3, 5, or 7?

800. Junior Showmanship Classes were originally developed as Children's Handling Classes at US dog shows. When were they first introduced?

801. When was the first all-breed licenced obedience test held in the US? Was it 1906, 1936, or 1956?

802. What is the top award for a Junior Handler in the US?

803. Who was the first woman judge in GB?

804. What is meant by the term "All-rounder"?
805. When did the AKC first publish a judges directory, listing all judges with permanent licences, giving names, addresses, and breeds?
806. Which of the following countries has an apprentice judging system? Sweden, UK, and Australia
807. Which Australian kennel club was the first to launch a Judges Training and Examination Scheme?
808. Which is the largest dog show held in the Netherlands?
809. Which is the largest dog show held in France?
810. Which is the largest dog show held in Scandinavia?
811. Which is the largest dog show held in New Zealand?
812. Where was the World Dog Show held in 1994?

Chapter 6

Organisations

813. What do the initials FCI stand for?
814. What do the initials RSPCA stand for?
815. What do the intitials SSPCA stand for?
816. What do the initials ISPCA stand for?
817. What do the initials ISDS stand for?
818. What do the initials AKC stand for?
819. What do the initials BVA stand for?
820. What do the initials ANKC stand for?
821. What do the initials NZKC stand for?
822. Which British organisation is known in North America by the initials TKC?
823. What do the initials DWAA stand for?
824. Which is Britain's largest dog rescue charity?
825. Which is the oldest German Shepherd club or society in Britain?
826. Which was the first Old English Sheepdog Club formed in Britain?
827. What was the main purpose for forming The Alsatian, Sheep, Police and Army Society in 1923?
828. Which organisation is responsible for organising sheepdog trials in Australia?
829. What is the official name of the Beligian Kennel Club?
830. Which organisation is responsible for hunting in France?
831. France has 2 museums dedicated to hunting. Can you name one?
832. Which historic English castle holds a unique collection of dog collars?
833. Which British museum held "The Man's Best Friend" canine art exhibition in 1991?
834. In which British museum will you find a large collection of stuffed dogs?
835. Where would you have gone to see the "Fidos and heroes in bronze" art exhibition?
836. Which American breed club was formed on St Patrick's Day

1962, when a group of breed enthusiasts met in Brooklyn?

837. Name one of the 2 breed clubs which uses the dog depicted on the tomb of Antefa II (XI Dynasty) as their emblem?

838. Which breed is the official mascot of the US Marine Corps?

839. Which American organisation registers Coonhounds and sponsors their competitive events?

840. What was The Keeshond Club orginally called?

841. Which national kennel club maintains a 24-hour Dog Law telephone hotline, to deal with dog legislation enquiries?

842. What do the initials ADOA stand for?

843. Which US organisation promotes training for airline baggage handlers to ensure that dogs are transported safely and are well cared for?

844. Which organisation is the largest single breeder of dogs in Britain?

845. Which British dog charity launched an appeal in 1990 to finance a new kennel block, and had 37,700 building bricks which were given away in return for a £25 donation?

846. Which British organisation was established to find new homes for racing greyhounds once they were too old to run?

847. Which American hospital is dedicated to canine medicine alone?

848. What was the British Veterinary Association known as before 1952?

849. What is a PAT dog?

850. Which British dog charity provides free community services, including over 4,000 registered PAT dogs?

851. Police dogs were in common use throughout Europe and the US by 1900. When and by whom were dogs first used officially by a police force?

852. For which other armed service does the RAF train search dogs?

853. What is the aim of the organisation FRAME?

854. Hearing Dogs for the Deaf is a charity providing assistance dogs for the deaf. What are the dogs trained to do?

855. Which is older:- National Beagle Club (US) or The Beagle Club (UK)?

856. Who organises the Annual Sled Dog Race in Britain?

857. Who publishes a magazine called "The Howler"?

858. Which organisation was responsible for dogs being used in the Avalanche Search Association?

859. Who organised the first canine biathlon?

860. Which former British colony's kennel club was established in 1886, with Sir William Jervois, the Colonial Governor as its patron?

861. Which national kennel club publishes a magazine titled "Dogtalk"?

862. Which national kennel club publishes a magazine titled "Pure-bred dogs"?

863. Which kennel club was established in 1972 as a result of a split from the jurisdiction of the Malaysian Kennel Association?

864. What is the name of the governing canine authority in South Africa?

865. Which national kennel club has the initials VDH?

866. In which country would you find the Pietermaritzburg Kennel Club?

867. In which of the following cities is the Societe Cynologique Suisse (Swiss Kennel Club) located? Geneva, Berne, or Lucerne?

868. In which of the following cities is the Norsk Kennel Klub (Norwegian Kennel Club) headquarters located? Oslo, Bergen, or Stavanger?

869. In which of the following cities is the Israel Kennel Club's headquarters located? Jerusalem, Ramat Gan, or Haifa?

870. In which of the following cities is the Societe Centrale Canine pour l'Amelioration (French Kennel Club) headquarters located? Paris, Strasbourg, or Aubervillers Cedex?

871. In which of the following countries is the Canadian Kennel Club headquarters located? Ottawa, Toronto, or Vancouver

872. Which Australian kennel club is known by its initials RASKC?

873. Which kennel club represents the Australian Northern Territories?

874. In which country would you find the Pilbara All Breeds Kennel Club?

875. In which country would you find the Fremantle Dog Club?

876. Cumann na Gadhraidheachta Ghaedhlaigh is a national kennel club. What is it known as in English?

877. The 2nd World Congress of Kennel Clubs was held in Edinburgh in May 1981. What did it commemorate?

878. What is the Scandinavian Kennel Union?

879. When was the Kennel Club founded?

880. When was the American Kennel Club founded?

881. The National American Kennel Club was founded in January 1876, but changed its name in 1884. What was its new name?

882. What did the National Bench Show Association (of US) change its name to?

883. When was the Canadian Kennel Club founded?

884. Before the establishment of the Canadian Kennel Club to whom did the Canadian clubs look to for guidance and registrations? Great Britain, France, or America

885. When was the French Kennel Club (Societe Centrale pour l'Amelioration) founded?

886. Under whose jurisdiction does the Guernsey Kennel Club operate?

887. When did the Kennel Club celebrate its centenary?

888. When did the American Kennel Club move to its present address at 51 Madison Avenue, New York?

889. When did the Kennel Club move into its present address at Clarges Street, London?

890. When was the FCI established?

891. Where are the headquarters of the FCI located?

892. When did the Kennel Club begin to publish their Stud Book?

893. When did the American Kennel Club begin to publish their Stud Book?

894. When did the Irish Kennel Club publish the first volume of their Stud Book?

895. When was the National Coursing Club established in Britain?

Section 2

896. Which university pioneered the development of insulin treatment for diabetic dogs?

897. The Animal Medical Centre of New York consists of the Ellin Price Speyer Hospital and the Margaret M. Caspary Veterinary Research Institute. What percentage of its patients are dogs? Is it approximately 25, 50 or 70%?

898. Which navy has a tradition going back 200 years of naming sister ships Beagle and Bulldog?

899. In which year did the Royal Navy ban keeping mascot dogs on ships because of the threat of rabies? Was it 1919, 1977 or 1989?

900. Which was the first pioneering training centre for guide dogs/seeing eye dogs in the US?

901. The American Humane Society was founded in 1878. What was its original aim?

902. The world-famous Angell Memorial Animal Hospital in Boston is named after which animal-welfare campaigner?

903. Which British club founded in 1928 had within only 3 months enrolled 10,000 canine members?

904. Which British national newspaper used to be advertised as "The A1 paper for canine owners"?

905. Which international dog organisation was formed in 1993 to collaborate with other organisations in disaster relief, including the International Red Cross, and the UN Disaster Relief Organisation?

906. What is the National Working Dog Convention?

907. Which British dog-related organisation ran a national children's poster competition in 1993 with the theme -Safety on 6 legs?

908. What is JACOPIS?

909. Which annual international event includes a grooming competition and educational conference?

910. Two restrictions on the membership of the Scottish Kennel Club were introduced in 1882. One was that only gentlemen resident in Scotland could become members. What was the other?

911. In 1911, the National Coursing Club allowed a dog called

"Baz" to be registered in the Greyhound Stud Book. What was so special about "Baz"?

912. What do the initials COCA stand for?

913. Which American Kennel Club film won the Silver Screen Award of the the US Industrial Film Festival?

914. The first dog club anywhere in the world was founded in 1869, but only lasted a short time. What was its title?

915. What was the Order of the Pug?

916. Why does the Pug Dog Club (of GB) have orange as its official colour?

917. In Britain, which additional breed was first catered for by the Japanese Spaniel Club, and only established its own club in 1904?

918. Which British charity ran a quarantine kennel for the dogs of servicemen returning from the First World War, who could not afford the normal quarantine kennel fees?

919. Where was the first World Canine Congress held in 1936?

920. How many countries sent delegates to the First World Canine Congress in 1936?

921. Why was the Tibetan Breeds Association formed in Britain in 1934?

922. Which breed was allowed by the Kennel Club to be registered with the prefix O.E.M.C.?

923. Name one of the organisations which supports the general interests of dog handlers in the US?

924. Which is the parent club of the German Shepherd Dog, which has its headquarters in Augsburg, Germany?

925. Which is older the Deutscher Teckelklub or The Dachshund Club (UK)?

926. What was the Imperial Association, and when was it formed?

927. The Norwegian Goverment (Ministry of Defence) had the power to mobilise what type of dog, and why?

928. Which was the KGB's favourite breed of guard dog?

929. The Australian Native Dog Training Society is based in New South Wales. What is the main objective of the Society?

930. Which organisation has the motto "A fair go for our Dingo"?

931. Which national organisation formed the Committee for National & Forgotten Breeds in 1974, to stop the decline in certain of its native breeds?

932. Who formed the Society for the Preservation of Japanese Dogs and why?

933. The Jack London Club was a famous animal welfare organisation. What did it protect?

934. The Bell Mead Kennels in Berkshire were originally only a teaching centre for kennel work when established in 1924. They are now famous for being the country annex for convalescent dogs from which rescue organisation?

935. In November 1980, a meeting was held between various national kennel clubs to discuss the possible unification of breed standards. The organisations included the Kennel Club, the American Kennel Club, and the FCI. Which other national organisation was invited, but was unable to attend?

936. In 1907, a British organisation was formed to regulate the sport of racing trail hounds. What is it called?

937. Does the American Kennel Club have individual membership?

938. Does the Kennel Club have individual membership?

939. What did training schools at Oldenburg (1916), Wurttemberg (1917) and Plessis-Trevisse (1918) herald the start of?

940. In which year did the British Driver Vehicle Licensing Authority (DVLC) auction the special K registration number plates, including K9, K9 PAL, and K9 PAWS? Was it 1989, 1991 or 1993?

941. How often does the FCI hold its General Assembly?

942. Which national kennel club holds the chairmanship of the Asian Kennel Union?

943. When was the National Dog Week movement established?

944. Which is the controlling authority for greyhound racing in Britain?

945. Which is the second largest dog registration organisation in the US?

946. What is the famous museum called at the National Greyhound Association's headquarters in Abilene, Kansas?

947. When was the Spanish Kennel Club (Real Sociedad Central de Fomento de las Razas Caninas en Espana) officially established. Was it 1899, 1906, 1912?

948. Which American organisation publishes a magazine called "Bloodlines"?

949. The Spanish Kennel Club publishes the "Libro de origens Espanol". Is it the history of Spanish native breeds, the official Spanish Kennel Club stud book, or the history of the Spanish Kennel Club?

950. When did the New Zealand Kennel Club introduce a Challenge Certificate system. Was it 1886, 1900, or 1905?

951. Which is older the Danish or Norwegian Kennel Club?

952. Does the Canadian Kennel Club have individual membership or club membership?

953. Which British organisation established the "International Kennel Club" in 1900?

954. Which American organisation presents an annual "America's Dog Hero of the Year" award, the canine equivalent of the Congressional Medal of Honour?

Section 3

955. a. When was the first official meeting of the Australian National Kennel Control (ANKC) held? Was it 20th March 1939, 14th April 1949 or 6th December 1954?

b. Where was the ANKC meeting held? Was it the Royal Agricultural Society's Showground, Royal Easter Show; South Australian Canine Association's Show, Victoria Park Racecourse; or the Central Australian Annual Show, Alice Spring?

c. What responsibility does the ANKC have?

956. Australia has 8 canine authorities – 6 state and 2 federal authorities. Can you name 3?

957. The American Kennel Club accredits 4 types of club to conduct sanctioned matches, i.e. Specialty clubs. Name the other 3.

958. a. What event is regarded as the "Blue Ribbon of the Leash", and is the equivalent of the Derby horse race?

b. Where and when is it run?

959. a. What is the name of the governing body that controls greyhound racing in Eire – S. Ireland?

b. Which was the first greyhound racing stadium in the US?

c. Greyhound racing was introduced to France in 1933 but only had a short life before being suspended. When did it stop? Was it 1951, 1960 or 1965?

960. a. What is the American equivalent of the Royal College of Veterinary Surgeons in GB?

b. When was either the American or British body founded?

c. What role do both organisations share?

961. a. When and where was the 1st World Conference of Kennel Clubs held?

b. How many national delegates attended? Was it 30, 70 or 120?

c. What was the aim of the Conference?

962. a. When was The Dog Museum of America formally opened?

b. Where was it originally located?

c. Where is its present permanent home?

963. a. The American Kennel Club was established in 1884. Where was the inaugural meeting held?

b. How many attended the inaugural meeting? Was it 14, 25 or 38?

c. When did the AKC first publish a book of breed standards

964. a. The Kennel Club was established in 1873. Where was the inaugural meeting held? Was it Newcastle, Birmingham or London?

b. How many attended the inaugural meeting? Was it 14, 25 or 38?

c. When did the Kennel Club adopt a system of dog registration?

965. a. The American Kennel Club and The Kennel Club were

originally "men only" clubs. When did the AKC finally allow women to serve as delegates?

b. The Kennel Club did not allow women to become members, but formed a Ladies' Branch. When was this established?

c. When were women finally allowed to be elected as members of the Kennel Club?

966. a. In 1953, the American Kennel Club produced its first film. Name the title?

b. What was the film about?

c. The AKC had run a competition amongst the AKC staff to name the fim. Who won?

967. In 1984, the United States Postal Service produced four AKC centennial stamps honouring the sport of pure-bred dogs. The stamps featured 8 breeds, can you name 3?

968. a. When did the Kennel Club first publish a monthly magazine?

b. When did the American Kennel Club first publish a monthly magazine?

c. Which is the oldest sporting journal in the US?

969. a. The present Search and Rescue Dogs Organisation was developed during the Second Wold War. What specific role did the search dogs have?

b. In the 1960's the Royal Air Force began to be interested in using search dogs for which specific purpose?

c. It is important that people can instantly identify search dogs. How would you be able to identify an RAF search dog from an RAF patrol dog?

970. a. When did the Royal Air Force establish its first dog training school in GB? Was it 1917, 1940 or 1956?

b. Originally a variety of different breeds were trained at the school, but one breed took over. What breed is now chosen?

c. How are RAF dogs recruited?

971. a.   Which is the oldest animal protection society in the world?

b.   The organisation came into being as a result of a public meeting called at the Old Slaughter's Coffee House, London in June 1824. Who called the meeting?

c.   Who became the Royal Patron of the organisation?

972. a.   Name the American organisation which is the equivalent of the British "Hearing Dogs for the Deaf"?

b.   What rights does the organisation claim for its dogs?

c.   How can these dogs be immediately identified?

973. a.   ADAPT is a British charity which trains dogs to help the disabled gain independence. What is its full title?

b.   By what other title was the charity originally known as?

c.   The work of the charity is based on the world-famous Dutch assistance dog training organisation. Can you name it?

974. a.   What do the initials PDSA stand for?

b.   Where was the first clinc opened in 1917?

c.   What is the aim of the organisation?

975. a.   Which British animal charity was originally known as "Our Dumb Friends' League"?

b.   Where was its first veterinary hospital opened in 1906?

c.   Why does it use the sign of the Blue Cross as its logo?

976. a.   Which organisation governs coursing in Eire (southern Ireland)?

b.   When is the British coursing season?

c.   Which other country holds a Waterloo Cup race?

977. a.   British Whippet racing has 2 clubs, one of which was founded by The Whippet Club of England. Can you name it?

b.   Can you name the other club?

c.   What is the main difference between the clubs?

978. a. The US Department of Agriculture (USDA) has a
      Beagle Brigade which patrols one of the US's busiest
      foreign arrival points. Where is the Brigade based?
      b. What are the Beagles used for?
      c. How do the dogs indicate that they have success in their
      search?

Chapter 7

Personalities Questions

Section 1

The following chapters deals with individuals and their dogs, and people who have been influencial in the world of dogs. The characters may be fictional, human or canine.

979. Name the German tax collector who developed a guard dog breed which still bears his name?

980. Who owned a Cocker Spaniel called Flush?

981. Which famous English clergyman was admonished by his Bishop for spending too much time on his hunting and his dogs?

982. Who was John Peel of the song "D'ye ken John Peel?

983. Which famous personality was known as the canine Napoleon or the canine Barnum?

984. Who was responsible for the First Forest Laws, which restricted the types of dog which could kept by the population of England in 1016?

985. Who was Bernard of Menthen (923-1008), and why is he important to dogs?

986. Who was the first Chairman of The Kennel Club?

987. Who was the first President of the American Kennel Club?

988. Who was the first President of the Canadian Kennel Club?

989. Who was the first Chairman of the Australian National Kennel Control?

990. Who established the United Kennel Club in the US?

991. Which army General had a white Bull Terrier called Willie, who accompanied the troops during the 2nd World War?

992. Which army General is famous for defending his Cocker Spaniel by saying " . . . that is my chair and Blackie can get into it any time he wants to"?

993. Who was forbidden to keep a dog in his rooms at Trinity College, Cambridge University, so kept a bear instead?

994. Who owned a German Shepherd Dog called Blondi, and on April 28th 1945 tested out his cyanide capsules on the dog before committing suicide.

995. Name the first dog to be launched into space in Sputnik II, on 3rd November 1957?

996. Can you name 1 of the 2 astronaut dogs which were the first to survive and return from space?

997. The portrait artist, Sir Henry Raeburn painted which famous author with his greyhound, Percy?

998. Who said "I have so many dogs, that I think I should be Patroness of your Association" (Ladies Kennel Association)?

999. Which famous dog book author was the first Editor of the American Kennel Club's journal – the American Kennel Gazette?

1000. Which ancient Greek was nicknamed "The Dog" because he flouted social convention and "embraced shamelessness and poverty"?

1001. In 1931, the American millionairess, Ella Wendel left a record legacy in her will to her pet poodle, Tiby. How much was the legacy? Was it $1 million, $5 million or $15 million?

1002. The Australian Terrier did not become popular in GB until which British Governor-General bought one as a pet for his family in the 1930's?

1003. In 1960, Princess Margaret bought a toy dog as a pet, and called it Rowley. What breed was Rowley?

1004. Which important British family owned a Corgi called Dookie and a Tibetan dog called Choo-Choo?

1005. What prize did a dog called Pickles find under a bush in South London in 1966?

1006. Name the Jack Russell Terrier who became an international celebrity after "adopting" an army unit in Northern Ireland in the 1970s, and surviving 2 bomb blasts and numerous sniper attacks?

1007. Name the diabetic dog which was the first animal to survive on insulin?

1008. Who is the Gordon Setter named after?

1009. Which animal behaviourist has developed the Sirius puppy training and socialisation programme?

1010. Which American dog fancier commissioned a customised maroon Cadillac in order to take the dogs to shows in comfort. The car had 8 doors and could hold 12 dogs?

1011. Which British canine artist used the pseudonym "Mac" for her postcard illustrations?

1012. Which British TV broadcaster and writer gained nationwide popularity through presenting "One man and his dog" – the televised sheepdog trial competitions?

1013. Which 19th century British photographer specialised in animal photography, particularly dogs, and has become a household name associated with canine photography?

1014. Who were the first Englishmen to see Eskimo Dogs?

1015. Which British monarch is associated with the following quotation "God save your Majesty, but God damn your dogs"?

1016. Which explorer led a Trans-Arctic expedition across the polar ice-cap in 1968-9, using Siberian Huskies?

1017. How many dogs did Captain Scott take on his last expedition to the Anctartic? Was it 35, 45 or 55?

1018. With which breed do we associate Captain Max von Stephanitz?

1019. Which photographer produced the classic photographic sequences of dogs and other animals in motion?

1020. Which Russian scientist's experiments led to his theory on conditioning reflexes, which is the basis of modern dog training methods?

1021. Which famous Greyhound won 3 Waterloo Cups, and was presented at Court to Queen Victoria, in 1871?

1022. Who is credited with importing the first Japanese Akitas into the US in 1937?

1023. Who was responsible for importing the first Rottweilers into GB in 1936?

1024. Who founded the Swedish Kennel Club, and developed the Hamiltonstovare breed?

1025. The Magyars moved eastwards from the Urals to the central Danube plains in the 9th century, and brought with them their sheepdog – what breed was this?

1026. Mr Fuller, of Rosehill, Sussex, is recognised as the original breeder of which dog?

1027. Who owned the Queen's Head Tavern in London, where he ran the Toy Dog Club?

1028. The Nyam-Nyam tribe of West Africa had a breed of dog, which has found popularity in Britian and America. What is it called?

1029. Which 18th century French courtesan had 2 Papillons named Inez and Mimi?

1030. Gypsy Rose Lee, the famous striptease artist, helped popularise which breed of dog, when she bought one as a pet in the 1950s?

1031. Which famous American General travelled with a pack of 40 coursing dogs, and was racing his dogs the day before he left on his fatal expedition to Big Horn River in 1876?

1032. In the American War of Independence, George Washington declared a special flag of truce to return a valuable item to the enemy. What was handed over to the British Commander?

1033. Which famous American dogman and judge wrote a show critique which included the infamous quotation "The champion bitches were old matrons whose quondam charms are mostly fled"?

1034. Charles Cruft found fame as a dog show promoter, but what was his other job?

1035. Who was the longest serving President of the AKC?

1036. Who was the first President of The Borzoi Club in GB?

1037. Which breed did Theodore Roosevelt and Jimmy Carter both have as pet dogs?

1038. Which US President had a Weimaraner called Heidi?

1039. President John F Kennedy was presented with a canine gift from the Irish President Eamon De Valera? Can you name the dog or the breed?

1040. The Russian President Khrushchev gave President John F Kennedy an official gift of a dog called Pushinka. What was so special about her?

1041. President Lyndon Johnson was sent a white Collie as a present from a schoolgirl in Illinois. What did President say when he accepted the gift?

1042. Richard Nixon in his 1952 Checker speech, describes a canine present which was a post-election present from Texas, and was part of corruption allegations. What breed was the dog?

1043. Which breed of dog was named after Queen Henrietta of Belgium's home, the Chateau de Laeken?

1044. Which breed of dog is associated with John Churchill, 1st Duke of Marlborough?

1045. Who was the first westerner to bring back a Japanese Chin from Japan in 1853?

1046. Which breed of dog did General Lafayette bring to America in 1824, as a present for his friend, J S Skinner?

1047. Which breed of dog was a great favourite with the German Chancellor Bismarck, and William "Buffalo Bill" Cody?

1048. Which breed was a great favourite with Mrs William Randolph Hurst, and the boxing world heavyweight champion, Gene Tunney?

1049. In 1931, Zeppo Marx and his wife acquired 2 dogs in England (Asra of Ghazni and Westmill Omar). These dogs were the US foundation dogs for which breed?

1050. Which French novelist had a French Bulldog, which was immortalised in "Dialogues des Betes", written in 1904?

1051. Which American novelist's first book was about her pet Poodle, but found greater fame with a later book entitled "The Valley of the Dolls"?

1052. With which breed are the Hottentots, Cornelius Van Rooyes, and the Rev. Charles Helm associated with?

1053. With which breed is S F Mosely associated with ?

1054. In 1840, the Irish Wolfhound was virtually extinct. who is credited with reviving the breed by using Scottish Deerhound as an outcross?

1055. Which English King banned dogs from his court?

1056. Who was responsible for reviving English interest in the King Charles Spaniel?

1057. In 1903, which member of the Royal family blocked an attempt to change the name of the King Charles Spaniel?

1058. With which breed is Edward Laverack associated with?

1059. Which breed is Francis Redmond credited with establishing an uniformed type in the 19th century?

1060. Who was the first President of the Lakeland Terrier Club?

1061. Which American actor is a great fan of Lakeland Terriers, and is co-owner of many leading US top-winning dogs, including Welsh Terriers and Fox Terriers?

1062. Who developed an all-white strain of Bull Terrier, and showed his famous bitch Puss in 1862?

1063. Who invented the mechanical lure in 1912, which led to the development of greyhound racing in the 1920s?

1064. Who was reputedly bitten by his newly-wedded wife's pet dog, Fortune, when he entered Josephine's bridal bedchamber?

1065. Empress Elizabeth of Russia, wife of Tsar Nicholas II, had a favourite pet dog called Eira. What breed was it?

1066. Why did Morris Frank, the owner of the first Seeing Eye dog change the dog's name to Buddy?

1067. Who was Mick the Miller?

1068. Who is regarded as the originator of sheep dog trials?

1069. Which well-known dog trainer was responsible for training Hollywood dogs, including "Buck" in the film Call of the Wild, and "Toto" in The Wizard of Oz?

1070. Who maintained a kennel of Foxhounds at his home at Mount Vernon?

1071. Which English monarch said that the preferred a greyhound to a spaniel as the former had all the good nature of the other without the fawning?

1072. Which Chancellor of the Exchequer had a Jack Russell called Budget?

1073. Which English monarch popularised the Cairn Terrier, and was President of the Cairn Terrier Club?

1074. Who invented the name Finkie for the Finnish Spitz?

1075. Who bred small red terriers, which became popularly known as Jones Terriers, later named Norwich Terriers?

1076. Which artist often included his own dogs in his work, including Cracker, the Bull Terrier, and Micky the Irish Wolfhound?

1077. In 1814, Colonel Peter Hawker described a short-coated black water dog in Newfoundland, and named them St John's Newfoundland. What is the breed known as today?

Section 2

1078. William Wade was the first American to import a Borzoi into the US, but Elsie was imported from England. Who was the first American to visit Russia and import a Russian dog?

1079. Colonel Thorton's dog "Pitch" in the 1790s is regarded as the prototype for which breed?

1080. Which American sportsman was a member of the German Weimaraner Club, and imported the first pair of Weimaraners into the US in 1929?

1081. Who was responsible for producing the "Stud Book of the Duke of Buccleuch's Labrador Retrievers"?

1082. Who wrote "We always call mine Labrador dogs, and I have kept the breed as pure as I could from the first I had from Poole . . ."?

1083. The American Rat Terrier was developed from Smooth Fox Terrier and Manchester Terrier crosses. Who was responsible for naming the breed?

1084. Who was largely responsible for saving the Dogue de Bordeaux from extinction in the 1960s?

1085. Who was responsible for developing the Dogo Argentino?

1086. In 1949, Dr Frantisek Horak began crossing Scottish and Sealyham Terriers. Which breed did he develop?

1087. Who was Wilson "Bluetick Bill" Harshman?

1088. In 1905, Miss Hamilton-Fletcher visited Holland and fell in love with the Dutch barge dogs, which she began to import into GB. She became an important figure in the British dog scene, but was known by her married name of . . .?

1089. Who was largely responsible for organising the voluntary civilian agency "Dogs for Defense" in America in 1942?

1090. Which famous psychiatrist owned a Chow Chow called Jo-Fi?

1091. Who is responsible for intorducing mountain search and rescue dogs into GB, after attending an International Red Cross training course for Avalanche dogs at Engelbert, Switzerland?

1092. Who spent 18 months in an Eskimo village in the Arctic Circle studying the Malamute in the 1920's, and whose work forms the basis of most of breed history and pedigrees?

1093. Which French King was so fond of his toy dogs (Bichons) that he carried them wherever he went in a tray-like basket attached around his neck by ribbons. A custom which was quickly adopted by the ladies of the royal court?

1094. A portrait of King Henry the Pious of Saxony shows him with a Saluki, which is wearing a collar decorated with silver scallop shells. What does this signify?

1095. Who drew up the Scottish Deerhound breed standard, which was approved by the Deerhound Club in 1892?

1096. During 1940-47, the Bloodhound almost died out in GB, The Association of Bloodhound Breeders was reformed to try and correct the situation. Who provided a cross-bred Foxhound/Bloodhound bitch to help form outcross blood?

1097. Whose dog, Obo, was influential in the development of Cocker Spaniels?

1098. Who owned the Rivington Cocker Spaniels, which won at least 38 single stakes working titles between 1919-1939?

1099. In 1921 and 1925, 2 groups of Afghan Hounds were brought to England, and they formed the basis for the 2 distinct types which dominated the show scene for many years. Who introduced the Ghazni dogs from the north east of Afghanistan?

1100. Who introduced the southern Baluchistan Afghan Hounds into England?

1101. Which English family kept a distinctive type of springing spaniel, maintaining their own stud book from 1813 up until the 1930s, but with the breed becoming known as Springer Spaniels by 1900?

1102. What connect did the Duc de Noailles have with the Duke of Newcastle and Clumber Park?

1103. Who wrote about the Brittany "a maximum of quality in a minimum size"?

1104. Who bred Ch. Palmerston, regarded as the cornerstone of the modern Irish Setter?

1105. Tradition says that evety Labrador Retriever is descended from a mating of a dog called Tramp, and a bitch called Avon. Who owned Tramp?

1106. Who owned the Labrador Retriever bitch called Avon?

1107. In 1930, 3 dogs were brought to England from Tibet and were classed as Shih Tzus. Who brought the dogs to England?

1108. Who lived at Sutton Scarsdale, near Chesterfield, and spent 29 years writing the definitive book on early Pointer history?

1109. Who imported the first Standard Schnauzers into the UK, which were exhibited at Crufts in 1928?

1110. In 1775, George Cartwright named his own sled dog after a specific geographical area, and this name was later adopted as the breed name. Which breed?

1111. In 1778, Henry Pye devised a novel scheme for the classification of dogs. How did Pye divide them?

1112. Johannes Caius wrote the famous "De canibus Britannicis" in 1570, but writing dog books was a hobby not his livelihood. What was Caius's profession?

1113. In the mid 19th century, Prince Albrecht zu Solms-Bramenfels set about creating the ultimate "vorstehhund" or all purpose gundog. Which breed did he develop?

1114. The Sealyham Terrier derives its name from a country estate of Sealyham, near Haverfordwest in Wales. Who developed the Sealyham in his attempt to creat a strain of small dogs noted for its badger hunting ability?

1115. Who on a holiday to Florence, Italy in 1888, fell in love with a small white Pomeranian, called Marco, which was brought back to England and started a craze for the breed among society ladies?

1116. Julius Wipfel of Weinheim, Germany, is responsible for the creation of which breed?

1117. Who was Bally Shannon?

1118. Name one of the two men who are regarded as the founders of modern dog training?

1119. Who was one of the Illustrated London New's long serving artists, 1842-1900, who specialised in early dog and agricultural shows?

1120. The playwright J M Barrie owned both a Newfoundland and a St Bernard. How did he acquire the St Bernard?

1121. Which 18th century naturalist wrote in his diary of a pair of Chinese Chows that his new neighbour, who had been in the service of the East India Company, had brought home to England?

1122. Which zoologist was responsible for organising the famous exhibition of domesticated animals at the Natural History Museum, London in the early 1900s, and which formed the basis of the Museum's collection of dogs?

1123. Which Austrian animal behaviourist made extensive studies of dog behaviour, and published the successful "The Dog and Man"?

1124. Who published in 1939, his theory that the Weimaraner was a mutation of the now extinct St Hubertus Brachen?

1125. "Stubby" served in the 1st World War, was awarded the rank of Sergeant, and became the most decorated war dog in America. What breed was Stubby? Was it a German Shepherd Dog, an American Staffordshire Bull Terrier or a Labrador Retriever?

1126. Which Parisian theatre director claimed to have succeeded in compiling a "dog dictionary"?

1127. Who came from Long Island, USA, to England with her two King Charles Spaniels, "Ashton Defender" and "Ashton Rollo", and did much to develop colour and type in the breed?

1128. Whose mistress was reproached for attending mass in the "company of a madman, a monkey, and a barbet"?

1129. Which German soldier was always accompanied by a Greyhound called Azar, and served with George Washington in the American War of Independence?

1130. Which French naturalist believed that "the dog represented the most total conquest the human species had ever made over the animal world, exemplifying every kind of courage and loyalty elicited for no other motives than those of gratitude and love"?

1131. Who founded the office of "Master of the Royal Game of Bears and Mastiff Dogs" in England?

1132. Which monarch had a dog called "Jowler", who once had a letter tied to his collar asking the King to stop hunting and go home before the countryside was ruined?

1133. Which Scottish Bishop was described as a "collie", who "like a dog, keeps dropping into dinner uninvited"?

1134. In the 17th century, witchcraft and magic were powerful fears felt throughout society. Witch-finders were used to track down witches. Which famous English witch-finder used dog familiars, called Jamara and Vinegar, to seek out the witches?

1135. Which composer used a Bulldog called Dan, as his inspiration for one of his musical portraits in his "Enigma Variations"?

1136. Which composer/conductor when his concert was broadcast on the radio, would finish the performance with a goodnight message to "Marco", his spaniel, who would be listening at home?

1137. In 1944, just prior to D-Day, what Order was issued by General Eisenhower regarding army cats and dogs?

1138. Mrs Van Thaden was the first woman President of the Federacion Canofilia Mexicana (FCM) in 1977. What did she become?

1139. Name the Mayor of German town of Leonberg, who created a breed to represent the heraldic dog featured in the town's crest?

1140. Which Maryland resident's diary and records include the first mention of hounds being kept to chase fox in America, in 1650?

1141. Who was Secretary of the Toy Spaniel Club, one of the founders of the Schipperke Club in Brussels, and was the English Secretary of the Societe Royale St Hubert and the Klub Cynophelia of Holland?

1142. In the early 19th century, 2 strains of English Pug were dominant – the Morrison and the Willoughby. Who was Willoughby?

1143. Who is regarded as the father of the Basset Hound in Britain, and imported "Model", the first Basset shown at a British dog show?

1144. Which lawyer, later to become a US Senator, is remembered for his closing speech in the Old Drum case, the "most celebrated dog case ever tried in Johnson County, Missouri - or the world", and which became an eloquent eulogy to the dog?

1145. Who was responsible for domesticating the Canaan Dog, and training the breed as a guard dog for kibbutzs, mine detection, and as guide dogs?

1146. Which American surgeon perfected his technique and manoever to expel objects lodged in the throat of choking victims, by using Beagles?

1147. Which husband and wife team provided a President of the Richmond Dog Show Society and a President of the Kennel Club?

1148. Which husband and wife team successfully ran the Richmond and Windsor Championship Dog Shows from the 1960's to the 1980's?

1149. Name the individual who wrote under the pen-name of Stonehenge?

1150. Name the individual who wrote under the pen-name of Idstone?

1151. Name the individual who wrote under the pen-name of Canis?

1152. Name the individual who wrote under the pen-name of Ashmont?

Section 3

The following questions are multi-part, comprising of 3 sections. The aim is to identify the famous individual – human or canine, real or fictious, and name them. If the identity of the individual is known after the first clue, a maximum of 3 points are scored. If the identity is known after 2 clues are given, then 2 points are awarded, etc.

1153. Who am I?
a. I was owned by Mary, Queen of Scots.
b. I was inseparable from her, and hid under her skirt at her execution.
c. I was taken by one of my mistress's French ladies in waiting, as a memento, and was taken to France.

1154. Who am I?
a. I was a Skye Terrier, and was owned by a shepherd called John Grey.

b. I followed my master's coffin to his grave, where I remained for the next 14 years.

c. A monument was erected to my memory by the churchyard in Edinburgh.

1155. Who am I?

a. I was owned by a famous English poet.

b. I died in 1808, and my master wrote a poem commemorating my loyalty.

c. My master built a funerary monument to me at his ancestral home at Newstead Abbey.

1156. Who am I?

a. I am a Springer Spaniel.

b. I lived with my family at the White House.

c. I co-wrote a book about my life at the White House, and my master's life as President of the United States.

1157. Who am I?

a. My father was a pugilist, and later owned the Swiss Cottage Public House in north London.

b. I shall be remembered developing the Fox Terrier type in the late 19th Century.

c. I became the Chairman of the Kennel Club.

1158. Who am I?

a. I founded the Golden Retriever Club.

b. I strongly advocated working rather than show dogs, and condemned "shoe bench loungers".

c. I produced the 1st breed Champion – Ch. Noranby Campfire.

1159. Who am I?

a. I was born in Ireland, but spent most of my life at Ettington Park, Warwickshire.

b. I was influential in the development of the Flat Coated Retriever.

c. I was the first Chairman of the Kennel Club.

1160. Who am I?
a. I was a Bullmastiff, and was owned by an novelist.
b. I lived with the family at Haworth, Yorkshire.
c. My portrait was painted by one of the family, and I was portrayed in my mistress' novel "Shirley", in which I was called Tartar.

1161. Who am I?
a. I was a St Bernard from the Hospice of St Bernard in the Swiss Alps.
b. I saved 40 lives between 1800 and 1810.
c. I am preserved as a stuffed specimen at the Berne Natural History Museum.

1162. Who am I?
a. I was a German Shepherd Dog, and was rescued from a German dugout by American airmen, during the 1st World War.
b. I was taken back to America, where I was trained as a police dog.
c. I went to Hollywood and made 40 films, earning more than a million dollars.

1163. Who am I?
a. I was a Cocker Spaniel, and lived with my family in Wimpole Street, London.
b. I was given as a present to my mistress, by her friend Mary Russell Mitford.
c. I was kidnapped by dog thiefs, and my mistress paid £50 for my return.

1164. Who am I?
a. I lived at and kept my kennels at Guishachan, Invernesshire, Scotland.
b. I was a banker, and was known as Sir Dudley Majoriebank before being raised to the peerage.
c. I was influential in the development of the golden Retriever.

1165. Who am I?

   a. I was bought as a puppy by young Jolyon.

   b. I was a friendly, cynical mongrel, part Russian-Poodle, part Fox terrier.

   c. I lived for 18 years, and died at Robin Hill.

1166. Who am I?

   a. I was a miniature black poodle, and I was owned by a famous British politician.

   b. I lived at 10 Downing Street.

   c. I attended war cabinet meetings, and travelled with my master wherever he went.

1167. Who am I?

   a. I was born at the Daisy Hill Puppy Farm.

   b. I run a catering service under the pseudonym of Joe Cool.

   c. My owner is called Charlie Brown.

Section 4

The following dogs are important in the history of specific breeds. Can you identify the breed?

1168. Ch Brackenacre The Viking.
1169. Ch Dokham Cavadossi of Tintavon.
1170. Ch Irywill Wagga Wagga of Colom.
1171. Ch Birling Painted Lady.
1172. Sh Ch Golden Tint of Treqwillym.
1173. Ch Finchwood Irish Mist.
1174. Ch Briarghyll Camilla.
1175. Ch Little Gent of Hadleigh.
1176. Sh Ch Danaway Debonair.
1177. Ch Olac Moon Pilot.
1178. Ch Ginger Christmas Carol.
1179. Ch Montravia Tommy Gun.
1180. Ch Burtonswood Tommy Gun.
1181. Ch Honey King of Quatt.

1182. Ch Sternoc Kiki.
1183. Sh Ch Russetmantle Paris.
1184. Ch Dandyhow Shady Knight.
1185. Ch Stonebar Sebastian.
1186. Ch Luke Lively at Deansgate.
1187. Ch Astrellita The Silversmith.
1188. Ch Cluneen Adam Adamant.
1189. Ch Toast of Armstead.
1190. Ch Blackwell Ravelsaye Recruit.
1191. Ch Greenmount Greensleeves.
1192. Ch Deepridge Mintmaster.
1193. Am Ch & Sh Ch Homestead's Tiffany with Boduf.
1194. Ch Apposyte Montecalvo's Little Whiz II.
1195. Am & Can Ch Snow Dumpling Aphrodite.
1196. Ch Hillprize Kelli Sandra.
1197. Am, Can, Cuban & Mexican Ch Honey Creek Vivacious.
1198. Ch Andronicus Birtley.
1199. Ch Blondie Beautie.
1200. Ch Holly Lane's Windstorm.
1201. Am & Eng Ch Shalfleet Socialite.
1202. Ch The Mad Hatter O'BJ.
1203. Ch Wildemoor's Roberta Kay.
1204. Ch Greta von Herrenhausen.
1205. Ch Branded's First Endeavour.
1206. Ch Cordova Mishka of Baronoff.
1207. Ch Treyacres Katie-Did-Did-It.
1208. Ft Ch Tiger of Clipper City.
1209. Ch Halbury Jean of Arken.
1210. Ch Kentwood Dilys.
1211. Ch Charlie's Chablis o'Prophet.
1212. Am & Can Ch G'veret Kahlbah de Strathcona.
1213. Bella's Clara.
1214. Janeph Jill.
1215. Colerado Jumping Gypsy.
1216. Lejo's Hale of Phaedrian.
1217. Asra of Ghazni.

Chapter 8

Literature, the Arts and Media Questions

Section 1

1218. Who wrote The Hound of the Baskervilles?

1219. The Incredible Journey by Sheila Burnford was made in to a film. What was the film called?

1220. Name the Golden Retriever in The Incredible Journey?

1221. In the novel 101 Dalmatians, a foster mother was found for the puppies. What was her name?

1222. In the novel 101 Dalmatians, what breed of dog was the Colonel?

1223. Name Dennis the Menace's dog.

1224. Name the canine children's nanny in "Peter Pan".

1225. In the Walt Disney film Lady and the Tramp, what was Tramp doing when he was wrongly accused of attacking the baby?

1226. Which group of dogs have been called the descendants of the goddess Diana's dogs?

1227. Who said "Anyone who hates dogs and children can't be all bad"?

1228. Who wrote the song "Mad dogs and Englishmen go out in the midday sun"?

1229. Name the dog in Punch and Judy shows.

1230. Who wrote "A man's best friend is his dog"?

1231. What was the name of cowboy Roy Roger's dog?

1232. Which film opens with the Dog Frisbee Championships of Florida, 1978?

1233. Which children's novel features Chateau Bow-Wow?

1234. Who wrote:-
    "Brothers and sisters, I bid you beware
    Of giving your heart to a dog to tear"?

1235. Who wrote the poem:- "Elegy – the death of a mad dog"?

1236. Who wrote "A visit to Dog Land"?

1237. In folklore, the magician Merlin had what type of dog?

1238. In folklore, what did a howling dog predict?

1239. In Irish folklore, what should a maid not do on her wedding day?

1240. Which Roman god and what animal were the deities which protected the Roman home?

1241. Which Indian tribe believes that they are descended from a dog who fell to earth from the sky?

1242. Who was Cerberus?

1243. In the 13th century, it was a common belief that a dog could detect . . . what?

1244. Who wrote the novel "Lassie Come Home"?

1245. Flaubert's fictional character Madame Bovary loses her dog when travelling by coach. What breed was it?

1246. Whose dog jumped overboard and swam ashore with his master when their ship went down, and both spent many years shipwrecked on a desert island?

1247. Who were the Fluppy Dogs?

1248. Name the programme hosted by Micky and Minnie Mouse, Professor Ludwig von Drake and others which was an hour long tribute to dogs, featuring film clips from favourite dog scenes and cartoon characters?

1249. In the TV series M*A*S*H*, Capt B.J. Hunnicut often talked about his pet dog back home in the US. Can you name the dog?

1250. In the "Incredible Detectives" cartoon, Davey Morrison is kidnapped and his 3 pets track down his whereabouts. His pets are Madame Cheng, a Siamese cat; Henessy, a black crow; and Reggie the dog. What breed of dog is Reggie?

1251. Steven Spielberg's "Amazing Stories" TV series features an episode which tells the story of a suburban family dog, seen from the dog's point of view. Name the title of the episode?

1252. Which 1960's canine rock and roll duo parodied The Beatles?

1253. In the Tom and Jerry cartoons, what is the name of the dog who is Tom's great enemy in the neighbourhood?

1254. In the Disney cartoon film "Robin Hood", the characters appear as different animals i.e. Prince John is a lion. What animal is Robin Hood and Maid Marion?

1255. Who wrote the novel "The plague dogs"?

1256. Which film is set in the canine world of New Orleans in the late 1930's, in which the hero is a German Shepherd Dog called Charles B Barker?

1257. Which cartoon film tells the story of two unlikely friends, a fox cub and a hound puppy?

1258. In which Sherlock Holmes story was the mystery solved because of the curious incident of the dog that did nothing in the night-time?

1259. Ancient writers tell how Julius Caesar invaded Britain to obtain gold, horses, slaves and . . . ?

1260. Dogs are often depicted in English coats of arms. Which is the oldest type of dog found on a coat of arms?

1261. What is the heraldic term for a dog depicted with its nose to the ground?

1262. According to the chronicler Froissart, what did King Richard II's Math, his favourite Greyhound, do when the King was about to be deposed?

1263. According to Canon Law, what dog-related activities were the clergy forbidden to take part in?

1264. Which famous column in Rome depicts dogs fighting in armour?

1265. What are the "dog days"?

1266. "A traveller, by the faithful hound,
half-buried in the snow was found"
Which breed of dog was Longfellow writing about?

1267. Who wrote the novel "Jock of the Bushveldt"?

1268. Who painted a portrait of Prince Albert with his favourite Beagle hounds?

1269. Who wrote the "The Scottish Deerhound", the classic book on the breed published in 1892?

1270. When did Japan celebrate the "Year of the Dog"?

1271. Name the painting by Francis Barraud that has become a famous music trademark.

1272. What happened to John Steinbeck's first draft of his novel "Of mice and men"?

1273. "Freeway" is the name of the pet dog featured in which American TV series?

1274. What is the name of the Bloodhound in the cartoon film "The Aristocats"?

1275. Who had a hit record with "How much is that doggie in the window" in 1953?

1276. Which David Bowie hit record has a doggy song title?

1277. Who sang "I love my dog"?

1278. Which variety hall performers had a musical hit with "The little dog laughed" in 1939?

1279. In the 1960s which pop group had a doggy name?

1280. Which American rap singer has a canine name, based on his childhood nickname?

1281. Name Charles Schultz's own dog who became the inspiration for his famous Beagle character in the Peanuts cartoons.

1282. Name the dog in Walter Lorraine's book "The Dog Who Thought He Was A Boy?

1283. What is the book "Adventures plaisantes de Madame Gaudichon et de son chien" better known as?

1284. What was Old Mother Hubbard's dog called?

1285. Which breed became a Royal Navy mascot after being a popular pet aboard many ships?

1286. Who wrote "It is surely not for nothing that Rover is dog's most common name . . ."?

1287. Who wrote in a letter "Histories are more full of examples of the fidelity of dogs than of friends"?

1288. Who wrote "a dog's best friend is his illiteracy"?

1289. Which famous playwright said "I like a bit of mongrel myself, whether it's a man or a dog; they're best for everyday"?

1290. Sir Walter Scott wrote the following memorial tribute to his deerhound Maida.
"Beneath the sculptured form
which late you were,
Sleep soundly, Maida, at your
Master's door"
The inscription is on a monument which was placed at the front door of Scott's country home. Name the house.

1291. In which book of the Bible would you find the following quotation "a living dog is better than a dead lion"?

1292. In Greek mythology, who was turned into a stag by Artemis, and devoured by his own dogs?

1293. Hermes is best known as the guardian of flocks and cattle. What other animals did he protect?

1294. Who was T'ien Kow?

1295. In Dr Seuss's children's story "Hop on Pop", what is the name of the dog?

1296. Who was Laughing Gravy?

1297. Name the dog that appeared in Charlie Chaplin's film "A dog's life" in 1918.

1298. Which cartoon veterinarian travels to his patients on a pogo stick?

1299. Which cartoon dog drives a pink 1956 Cadillac, and has a "cool" gang of canines?

1300. Deputy Dawg is a not too bright Southern lawman. Where does this cartoon canine maintain law and order?

1301. Does the villanous Dick Dastardly and his fumbling hench-dog Mutley ever catch Yankee Doodle pigeon in their cartoon adventures?

1302. Which American TV series featuring a young boy and his talking dog was funded by the Lutheran Council of Churches?

1303. Tim Barton's cartoon film "Nightmare before Christmas" features a dog called Zero. What is special about Zero?

1304. Felix the Cat's arch enemies were the Professor and his Bulldog assistant. What was the dog's name?

1305. Name the dog that is Woody Woodpecker's greatest enemy.

1306. Agatha Christie's fictional detective Poirot is given a Wire-haired Terrier as a present in "Poirot loses a client". Can you name the dog?

1307. Spit is a glove puppet dog, and he is one half of a well-known comedy act. Can you name Spit's partner?

1308. Richmal Compton's wrote many stories about "Just William". Can you name William's dog?

1309. Name Cinderella's dog in the Disney film.

1310. Name the cartoon series with a dog who has a genius level IQ , and which has the catchphrase "Every dog should have a boy".

1311. Name the dog in the TV series "The Ghost and Mrs Muir".

Section 2

1312. Who wrote "Love me, love my dog"?

1313. Which English lexicographer gave the advice that barking dogs seldom bite?

1314. Which American author wrote "If you pick up a starving dog and make him prosperous, he will not bite you. This is the principal difference between a dog and man"?

1315. John Steinbeck wrote "If manners maketh man, manners and grooming maketh . . . "?

1316. James Thurber wrote of his dog "There was a slight advantage to being one of the family, for he did not bite the family as often as he bit strangers"? What breed of dog was Thurber's pet?

1317. Who wrote "Un drole de menage" in 1948, which describes how a family dog raises the children of Lord Sun and Lady Moon?

1318. In P G Wodehouse's novel "Mike and Psmith", who has long legs, a tenor voice, and was apparently made of India-rubber?

1319. In which novel was it "A wicked thing to start dog stories among a party of average sinful men. Let one man tell a dog story, and every other man in the room feels he wants to tell a bigger one"?

1320. Which is the first written reference to the Basset Hound?

1321. Which was the first printed dog book written in English?

1322. Which was the first dog book to be published in Scotland?

1323. Which 19th century author wrote of "canaille" or "doggery"?

1324. In which book would you find the literary cur, the nautical cur, curs of great expectations, and curs of the fancy?

1325. Who assisted Dido to write "One dog and her man"?

1326. Who wrote:-

"Where are the dogs going?
    you people who pay so little
    attention ask. They are going about their business.
    And they are vey punctilious, without wallets,

notes. . . and without brief-cases".

1327. Name the Clampett's dog in the TV series "The Beverly Hillbillies".

1328. Which fictional character describes an attack by a Scottish Terrier, as a great moment in a Greek drama, where someone is unconscious that Nemesis is at his heels?

1329. Who wrote:-
"You ask of my companions. Hills, sir, and the sun-down and a dog as large as myself that my father bought me. They are better than beings, because they know, but do not tell".

1330. Who said "If dogs could talk, perhaps we could find it as hard to get along with them as we do with people"?

1331. Who wrote:-
"It was not a beauty. All too obviously, it was a living souvenir of a mother who had never been able to say no. . . there was a suggestion of Sealyham Terrier about it, but that was almost blotted out by hosts of reminiscences of other breeds. It looked, on the whole, like a composite photograph of popular dogs!"

1332. Who was Charles Le Chien's, or rather, an old French gentleman poodle known as Charley, travelling companion?

1333. In Rupert Brooke's poem "The little dog's day", what did the little dog pray for?

1334. In which novel was a fictional pedigree provided for a stolen dog, which said the dog came from the Von Bulow kennels at Leipzig; his father was Arnheim von Kahlsberg, who had won 1st prize at the Berlin Exhibition in 1912; his mother was Emma von Trautensdorf, who was awarded a gold medal at the Nurnberg Thoroughbred Dog's Society?

1335. In which novel do you find the characters Buck, Sheet, Nig and John Thorton?

1336. Who wrote:-
"At night, my wife and I did fall out about the dog's being put down in the cellar, which I had a mind to have done because of his fouling the house, and I would have my will; and so we went to bed and lay all night in a quarrel".

1337. Who wrote about dogs "How odd that people of sense

should find any pleasure in being accompanied by a beast who is always spoiling conversation"?

1338. In which novel did an American visitor to Britain reply "I want to see the Beefeaters; and Cruft's Dog Show; and your blood horses; and the Derby", when asked if there was any particular thing he wished to see during his stay?

1339. Which Sherlock Holmes story features the Shoscombe spaniels, the most exclusive breed in England, which are talked about at every dog show?

1340. Which Roman author (c.63-21BC) wrote of the export of luxury hunting dogs from Britain?

1341. Pliny the Younger (23-74AD) mentions the training of dogs for what type of work?

1342. Dame Juliana Berner described in "The Boke of St Albans", 1486, the ideal example of a breed as "Head like a snake, necked like a drake, footed like a cat, tailed like a rat, sided like a bream, chined like a beam"? Which breed was she describing?

1343. In which Canterbury Tale, are Spaniels mentioned?

1344. Who wrote "Sir, a woman's preaching is like a dog's walking on his hinder legs. It is not done well, but you are surprised to find it done at all"?

1345. What was the name of Abram V Courtney's faithful dog who acted as his guide, companion, and bodyguard?

1346. Who wrote "Nature never makes a ferret in the shape of a mastiff"?

1347. Who wrote "The Uses of a Dog"?

1348. Can you identify the breed described as follows:-
"A pet. . . whose squat figure, black muzzle and tortuosity of tail that curled like a head of celery in a salad bowl, bespoke his Dutch extraction".

1349. Virginia Wolf's biography "Flush" records whose courtship?

1350. Who wrote "every dog has his day"?

1351. Who said "If a dog will not come to you after he has looked you in the face, you ought to go home and examine your conscience"?

1352. In which Shakespeare play would you find the following quotation?

"Thou callest me a "dog" without a case;
But since I am a dog – beware my fangs"

1353. In which Shakepeare play would you find the following quotation?
"My hounds are bred out of the Spartan kind, so flewed, so sounded; and their heads are hung with ears that sweep away the morning dew".

1354. In which Shakespeare play would you find the following quotation?
"Pish for thee, Iceland Dog. Thou prick-eared cur of Iceland".

1355. In which Shakespeare play would you find the following quotation?
". . . you may stroke as gently as a puppy greyhound".

1356. In which Shakespeare play would you find the following quotation?
"That island of England breeds very valiant creatures: their mastiffs are of unmatched courage".

1357. In which Shakespeare play would you find the following quotation?
"Cry "Havoc" and let slip the dogs of war".

1358. Why is St Godfrey of Amiens usually portrayed with a dead hound at his feet?

1359. Which saint is often depicted as a pilgrim with a dog beside him?

1360. What traditional ceremony was carried out on St Roche's feast day (August 16th)?

1361. What did Richard II's Game Laws prohibit a labourer or layman "which hath not land or tenemented to the value of 40/-, nor any priest or clerk, if he be not advanced to the value of £10 per annum from doing?

1362. In Anglo-Saxon Britain, what was hunted as a form of royal taxation?

1363. The religious Code of Cluny (1485) complained that "dogs defile monasteries". What specific crimes were held against dogs?

1364. In Greek legend, who was Argus?

1365. The Maoris have an ancient tattoing pattern called Moko Kewi (pattern of the dog). What is its origin?

1366. Irish folklore tells of a running race between a cat and a dog. What was the result of the race?

1367. Traditional tales regarding Noah's Ark give 2 different explanations as to why a dog has a cold nose. Can you give either explanation?

1368. Why did the Hebrews vilify dogs?

1369. According to the historian Herodotus, what did an ancient Egyptian family do when their pet dog died?

1370. What was the significance of the appearance of the dog star Sirius to the ancient Egyptians?

1371. In Irish folklore, which hound was so highly prized that fortunes, land, slaves and even 6000 head of cattle were offered to the Kings of Connaught and Ulster for him?

1372. The ancient Romans had separate descriptive names for horse dogs, shepherd dogs, sporting dogs, war dogs, fighting dogs for the arena, scent hunting dogs, and sight hunting dogs. True or false?

1373. The ancient Egyptian city of Cynopolis (the city of the dog) was built in honour of which god?

1374. In Indian mythology, why do black dogs have a special significance?

1375. The Siberian Eskimos believe that Ravan and his wife created reindeer out of the hair on their hands, and dogs from ...?

1376. Aelic in his ancient treatise on dogs wrote of a temple where huge dogs larger than Molossian hounds were sacred to the god Adranus, who at night would lead drunks safely home. Where was the temple?

1377. What do the Lamas of Tibet believe that pariah dogs are?

1378. In northern India, which dogs are believed to be inhabited by the spirit of the dead?

1379. Which native North American Indian tribe believe that Nagaicho, the creator of the world, had a dog which accompanied him whilst he worked.

1380. The Aztec Indian Xoloti was both dog and god. He was the faithful dog of the sun, and as such was responsible for what special task?

1381. Which breed is supposedly the result of a cross between the great Celtic hounds and a mongoose, and whose offspring were saved from culling by St Patrick?

1382. What are Yeth Hounds?

1383. Whose pet Poodle was accused in pamplets and newspapers of being his master's demonic familiar, and of teaching the King's children to swear?

1384. Who is the Mauthe dog?

1385. Who was Orthros?

1386. What Italian-French name for a mastiff is still used in heraldry to describe the representation of a "mastiff with cropped ears" on a coat of arms?

1387. Which 13th century Baron's seal and standard featured a Greyhound tied to the left stirrup of a knight, who is sounding a trumpet/horn?

1388. In Sir Edwin Landseer's painting "Dignity and Impudence", which 2 breeds look out on the world from their kennel?

1389. Which 19th century artist painted Princess Mary of Cambridge with her favourite Newfoundland?

1390. Which artist's first royal commission was to paint Queen Victoria's white Collie called Snowball?

1391. In 1573, the painter Veronese was summoned before the Inquisition to explain why his religious painting "The supper in the house of Levi" included unacceptable animals. What had Veronese included in his painting?

1392. In Titian's famous portrait of Duke Federigo Gonzaga of Mantua, the Duke is accompanied by his pet dog. What is the dog doing?

1393. Titian's painting "Adoration of the Magi" includes a dog. What is the dog doing?

1394. What miniature canine portrait was commissioned to be hung in Queen Mary's Dolls house at Windsor Castle?

1395. Which French artist was appointed by Louis XIV as the official painter of the Royal Hunt?

1396. Which famous 18th century portrait painter's first signed and dated (1745) painting was of a Bull terrier named Bumper?

1397. Who painted "A distinguished portrait of the Humane Society, which depicted a black and white Newfoundland?

1398. Which breed of dog features most frequently in Henri de

Toulouse-Lautrec's drawings and lithographs?

1399. Andy Warhol sometimes painted his own pets, a pair of miniature Dachshunds. Can you name them?

1400. Can you name Joan Miro's dog painting which was originally entitled "Toutou jappant la lune", but whose title was later changed?

1401. What is the name of the dog in the TV series "The Bionic Woman"?

1402. Which cartoon canine launched in 1959 was sponsored by Kellogg's, and in 1959 was the first animated cartoon to be awarded an Emmy by the Television Academy?

1403. The Poodle Polka, by Clarence C Corpi (1894) has few lyrics, but includes Bow-wow every few cords. True or false?

1404. Who wrote the song "Daddy wouldn't buy me a Bow Wow"?

1405. "Nimo the Wonder Dog" was a famous variety act. What was so special about Nimo's performances?

1406. Which American presidential archives have 11 boxes of official dog archives, entitled the "Fala file"? Is this from the Administration of Theodore Roosevelt, Franklin D. Roosevelt or Harry Truman?

1407. Which canine cartoon character was a spoof of Marlon Brando's role in The Godfather?

1408. Walter Lenz, best known for his creation of Woody Woodpecker, created an animated series featuring a young button-eyed boy and his faithful dog. The boy's name was Dinky Doodle, but what was his dog called?

1409. Which cartoon wolf and sheepdog adversaries start their day by clocking on duty by punching a time-clock, and break for lunch?

1410. What does the bronze statue of the Siberian Huskie "Balto" in Central Park, New York commemorate?

1411. In which architectural period would you find chiselled dog-tooth ornamentation?

Section 3

The following questions are multi-part, comprising 3 sections. Scoring is 1 point per correct answer to a maximum of 3 points.

1412. a. Who wrote: "All I observed was the silliness of the King playing with his dogs all the while, and not minding the business"
b. Who was the author talking about?
c. What breed of dog did the King have?

1413. a. Name the dog who accompanied Harris, George and Jerome on their boating trip on the Thames?
b. Name the author who wrote of their exploits on the Thames?
c. Did the dog accompany them on the bicycle holiday through the Black Forest, in the sequel of "Three men on the Brummel"?

1414. a. Which fictional character had a "sort of Dogs' College"?
b. What was the aim of the College?
c. What were the first pupils?

1415. a. In Arthur Conan Doyle's "A sign of four", why does Sherlock Holmes instruct Dr Watson to go to no. 3 Pinchin Lane which was a type of pet shop?
b. Who said "I would rather have Toby's help than that of the whole detective force in London"?
c. What was Toby?

1416. a. In Arthur Conan Doyle's "The hound of the Baskervilles" what type of dog was it?
b. Where was it bought?
c. Where was it kept on the moors?

1417. a. Who wrote: "The Dandie met him in the hall. Though he was not over-fond of dogs, the breadth and solidity of this one always affected Soames pleasurably - better than that little Chinese abortion they used to have!
b. What 2 breeds are described?
c. Who is Soames?

1418. a. Who wrote: " . . . You little devil. That dog is a proper little brute with strangers . . . I've known him bite clean through a lady's stocking. Francis Wilmot saw with interest a silver-grey dog nine inches high and nearly as broad looking up at him with lustrous eyes above teeth of extreme beauty"?
b. What breed is "the little devil"?
c. Who owns him?

1419. a. Who wrote the "Belle and Sebastian" stories for children?
b. Where were the stories set?
c. What breed of dog was Belle?

1420. a. In the novel "101 Dalmatians", what is the name of the owners of the Dalmatians?
b. What is the name of the villianess and her henchmen?
c. What did she want to do with all the Dalmatian puppies?

1421. a. Who wrote "101 Dalmatians"?
b. The author wrote a sequel. What was the title?
c. Who caused all living creatures apart from dogs, to go into a deep sleep and why?

1422. a. Rupert the Bear first appeared as a cartoon in 1936. Who created the character?
b. His friends included a Pekingese and a Pug. Can you name them?

1423. a. How many of Aesop's Fables feature dogs? Is it 3, 7 or 12.
b. What is the moral of Aesop's fable no. 46 "The dog in the manger"?
c. What is the moral of Aesop's fable no. 41 "The dog and the wolf"?

1424. a. Which novel tells the story of Eric, who one minute is an ordinary boy and the next he turns into a dog?
b. Who is the author?
c. Which breed of dog does Eric become?

1425. a.   Who was Dandie Dinmont?
     b. What did he call his dogs?
     c. Who is reputedly the inspiration for Dandie?

1426. a. James Thurber, the American humourist, wrote many articles and essays on his pet dogs which were published in which magazine?
     b. In which year was Thurber's "Men, Women, and Dogs" published?
     c. In which book did Thurber satirise pseudo-scientific sex manuals with a book based on a dog training manual?

1427. a. In which novel was Dorothea Brooke accompanied by her dog "who always took care of the young ladies in their walks"?
     b. Can you give the breed and the pet name of Dorothea's dog?

1428. a. In Aristophanes' play "Wasps" a dog is put on trial for what crime?
     b. Why is Alcibiades's dog often referred to as the first recorded docked breed?
     c. Which mythical hound was fated to catch whatever it pursued?

1429. In which Book of the Bible would you find the following quotations?
     a. The dogs shall eat Jezebel by the walls of Jezreel.
     b. The dogs eat of the crumbs which fall from their masters' table.
     c. The little foxes, that spoil the vine.

1430. Charles Dickens was very fond of dogs, and included dogs in many of his books. Can you name the owners of the following fictional dogs, and in which novel they appear?
     a. Diogenes.
     b. Ponto.
     c. Jip.

1431. Mongrels and crossbreds have their place in literature as well as the pure-bred. In which novel would you find thefollowing characters?
    a. The mongrel Garryowen?
    b. The mongrel Quoodle?
    c. The cross-bred Tartar?

1432. a. Who wrote:
    "The dog is a survival – an anchronism. He toils not, neither does he spin, yet Solomon in all his glory never lay upon a door-mat all day long, sun-soaked and fly-fed and fat, while his master worked for the means wherewith to purchase an idle wag of the Solomonic tail, seasoned with a look of tolerant recognition".
    b. The quotation is a parody of a passage from the Bible. Which one?
    c. What is the author's definition of a "cur"?

1433. a. Which was the first book on hunting to be written in English?
    b. When was it published?

    c. Which was the first printed dog book to be illustrated with coloured plates?

1434. Which modern poets wrote the following?
    a. "In the nightmare of the dark
       All the dogs of Europe bark."
    b. "Without silver light on their foliage
       the trees have grown larger
       and a horizon of dogs
       barked very far from the river."
    c. "Dogs display reluctance and wrath
       If you try to give them a bath.
       They bury bones in hideaways
       And half the time they trot sideways."

1435. Who wrote the following?
    a. "Dogmatism is puppyism come to its full growth".

b. "Men are generally more careful of the breed of their horses and dogs than of their children".

c. "When a dog bites a man, that is not news, because it happens so often. But if a man bites a dog, that is news."

1436. a. The Greek Goddess Hecate was often called the dog-headed death goddess, being depicted with 3 animal heads. What were they?

b. Hecate was considered to possess the bodies of which particular dogs?

c. What other form did she adopt apart from the 3-headed Goddess?

1437. a. What is the Celtic legend of Gelert?

b. Who gave Gelert as a present?

c. Where is Gelert buried?

1438. a. In Celtic folklore, whose canine footprints can be seen in the rocks at Builth in central Wales?

b. The legend of hunting the great boar Twrch Trwyth, tells of the hounds running from Ireland across the sea and through Wales. Where did the hunt end?

c. Tradition has it that King Arthur fed and water his dogs, at a famous Cornish landmark, where the rocks form natural hollows. What is the place called?

1439. a. In Irish folklore, Cuchulain is one of the greatest Celtic warriors. How did he acquire his name?

b. What taboo was placed on him?

c. What duties did Cuchulain acquire after he had killed the dog?

1440. a. In Germanic folklore, who had 2 wolves called Geri and Freki?

b. What was the Wild Hunt?

c. Sometimes one of the Wild Hunt was accidently left behind on the road or on the hearth of a household. What happened to the hound left on the hearth?

1441. a. In Greek mythology, Artemis was followed by a pack of hunting dogs, including dogs which Pan had given to her when she visited him in Arcadia. The dogs included 3 lop-eared hounds, 2 particoloured hounds, spotted hounds and what other type of dog?
b. What was a central feature of the festival held at the Temple of Artemis?
c. Who was the Roman equivalent of Artemis?

1442. a. In folklore, dogs are often depicted as field spirits, portecting the crops. Where is the most potent embodiment of this spirit to be found?
b. In France, what did they believe that the reaper of the last sheaf in a field had done?
c. In the Orkneys, what was the last sheaf or last load of grain called?

1443. In Granada, an old Spanish Christmas tradition tells of the 3 dogs that accompanied the shepherds to the stable to see the new-born Jesus. The names of these 3 dogs are still traditionally given to Granadian dogs. What are the 3 names? (1 point per correct answer)

1444. a. What did the ancient Romans believe that the housedog could do?
b. What did they often have by the entrance to the house, which is still preserved in Pompei?
c. What does the Roman motto "Cave canem" mean?

1445. a. Which continental porcelain factory was one of the earliest and best known for its Pugs?
b. Which English porcelain factory was best known for its Poodles?
c. Which English porcelain factory produced Doris Lindner's Sporting Dog series?

1446. a. The photographer and artist, William Wegman has used his dog in a successful series of post modernist photographs and videotapes. Can you name the breed and the dog's name?

b. Wegman's original dog was succeeded by whom?

1447. a. Which 18th century artist painted a self-portrait which included his pet Pug?
b. Name the dog?
c. In which Gallery is the painting is housed?

1448. a. Who was the creator of "Bonzo"?
b. Is it true that a well-known dog breeder sought the artist's advice in order to produce a new variety of dog to be called the Bonzo Terrier?
c. Bonzo the dog was one of the first neon signs to be put up in Piccadilly Circus, London. In which year did he appear?

1449. a. In the Chinese astrological calendar, which of the following years were the Chinese Year of the Dog? 1946, 1970, 1982 and 1994
b. Will the year 2006 be a Chinese Year of the Dog?
c. Which characteristics represent "The Dog" personality?

1450. a. In the French cartoon series, Asterix, who owns the dog?
b. What is the dog's English name?
c. What is the dog's original French name?

1451. a. What is the name of the dog featured in the book and film "The Thin Man"?
b. What breed was it in the original book?
c. What breed was it in the film?

1452. a. Who was Toto?
b. What breed of dog was used in the 1939 film?
c. What breed of dog was used in the 1976 sequel?

1453. a. Betty Boop, the bubbling beauty of the cartoon world was originally drawn in 1930. Betty was based on the actress/singer Helen Kane, and a breed of dog. Which breed?

b. The character was redrawn in 1932, when she appeared with companions. Can you name them?

1454. a. What was the inspiration for the "Road Runner and Wile E Coyote" cartoons?
b. It was designed as a parody of chase cartoons. From which viewpoint does the audience see the chase?
c. What does Wile E Coyote never do?

1455. a. Who is Scooby-Doo?
b. Which breed is Scooby?
c. Name his nephew?

1456. a. In the cartoon film "Lady and the Tramp", what breed of dog is Lady?
b. What is the name of the Scottish Terrier?
c. What breed is Caesar?

1457. a. Where can you find Almost-A-Dog Mountain?
b. Where can you find a lake called Lagua del Perro?
c. How did the Isle of Dogs in London acquire its name?

1458. International fashion designers have often used dogs as part of their logo designs.
a. Valentino uses a design based on his own pet dog called Oliver. What breed is Oliver?
b. Bella Freud's whippet Pluto is used as her design label. Which artist drew the caricature of Pluto?
c. Who's Greyhound advertises his own-brand aftershave and perfume?

1459. a. A bronze sculpture of a dog is situated in the entrance of the BBC Shepherd's Bush Television Centre. Which dog is commemorated?
b. Which year did she join the show?
c. Which other canine member of the cast had a popular song written about his exploits?

1460. a. What is St Hubert the patron saint of?

b. Which is his saint's day?

c. When is the Blessing of St Hubert invoked?

1461. a. Cynanthropy has two different meanings. Can you name them both? (1 point per correct answer).

b. What is lycanthropy more commonly known as?

1462. a. In which novel does Tolstoy describe a Russian wolf hunt using Borzois?

b. Who provides a detailed description of a year in the life of the hunt kennels in his "Memoirs of a Fox-hunting Gentleman".

c. Which Victorian artist painted 2 pictures recording the start and finish of a shooting holiday in Scotland, showing the shooting.party with their gundogs at St Pancras Station, London, and returning from Perth Station, Scotland?

1463. a. What breed of dog is Hooch in the movie "Turner and Hooch".

b. What breed of dog starred as the police dog in the movie "K9"?

c. What breed of dog is Ace's pet in the movie "Ace Venturer, Pet Detective"?

1464. Enid Blyton's children's stories often feature dogs. Can you give the missing dog's name from the following titles?

a. "_____ the Sheepdog".

b. "The Five Finder-outers and _____".

c. "The Adventures of _____".

1465. a. Who wrote the children's series "Spot the Dog"?

b. Who wrote and illustrated the children's story of a Sealyham Terrier in "Higglety-Piggelty-Pop"?

c. In Frank Muir's children's series, what breed of dog is "What-a-Mess"?

Chapter 9

Picture Questions

Looking at the diagram below . . .

1466. Where would you measure the height of a dog?
1467. Where would you measure the length of a dog?

Which of these foot illustrations show . . .

1468. Flat foot
1469. Cat foot
1470. Splay foot
1471. Hare foot

a

b

c

d

Picture Questions

2. Which of the following profiles show:

1472.   Dish face.
1473.   Brick face.
1474.   Ram's head face.
1475.   Wedge-shaped face.
1476.   Broken-up face.
1477.   Tapering face.

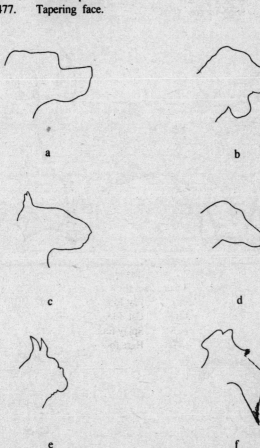

a   b

c   d

e   f

Which of the following ear illustrations show . . .
1478.   Semi-prick ears.
1479.   Tulip ears.
1480.   Prick ears.
1481.   Bat ears.
1482.   Propellor ears.
1483.   High-set rose ears.

a

b

c

d

e

f

Picture Questions

Which of the following front types
show . . .

1484.   Narrow front.
1485.   Cabriole front.
1486.   Wide front front.
1487.   Gun-barrel front.
1488.   Bandy front.
1489.   Pigeon-toed front.
1490.   Horseshoe front.

a

b

c

d

e

f

f

Which of the following tail illustrations show . . .:

1491.   Rat tail.
1492.   Gay tail.
1493.   Sickle tail.
1494.   Pump handle tail.
1495.   Flagpole tail.
1496.   Tufted tail.
1497.   Sabre tail.
1498.   Screw tail.
1499.   Bob tail.
1500.   Ring tail.
1501.   Feather tail
1502   Whip tail.

a

b

c

d

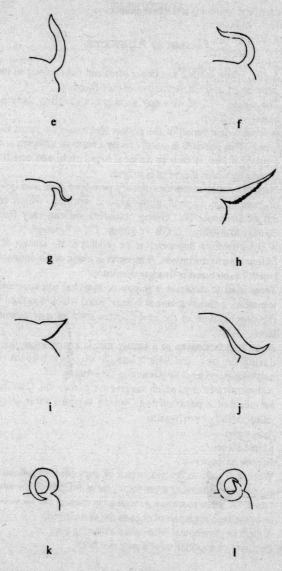

e

f

g

h

i

j

k

l

ANSWERS

General Answers

1. A dog whose mother and father (dam and sire) belong to the same breed, and are themselves of pure breeding.

2. The written record of a dog's ancestors covering three or more generations.

3. A written description of the perfect specimen of a particular breed. This standard is usually set by a national authority, i.e. a national kennel club or national breed club, and sets the criteria by which the breed is judged.

4. National canine authorities classify pure-bred dogs into types of breeds, i.e. hounds, gundogs, and working, which are called *Groups*. This Group classification can vary from country to country, i.e. GB – 6 groups; US – 7 groups.

5. A cross-bred is a dog which is the product of the mating of 2 different pedigree breeds. A mongrel is a dog of no definable breed, i.e. no breed is strongly dominant.

6. Term used to describe a puppy or dog that unexpectedly resembles a distant ancestral type or breed which was used in the development of the breed. Often used as a derogatory term.

7. A pet dog belonging to a family that is absent from home during the day, and which lets the dog out to roam the neighbourhood until they return in the evening.

8. A domesticated dog, which has reverted to the wild. Usually a member of a pack of dogs which support themselves independantly from humans.

9. A mongrel.

10. Iditarod Race.

11. Bejiing or Reykavik.

12. When it is used to describe a pair of dogs other than hounds. A couple is a hunting term for a pair of hounds of the same breed. A brace is a more general term used in the show ring or in the field for a pair of dogs of the same breed.

13. A sight or gaze hound, also called a running dog.

14. Purchase or importation of a pregnant bitch.

15. Someone with a bad temper.
16. Schipperke.
17. 480 metres
18. Keeping dogs out of the church and waking sleeping parishioners during church services. Some dog-whippers also had to keep the pulpit and church walls clean.
19. Corgi-Dachshund cross. The name was given to the cross-bred puppies which resulted from a mis-mating between one of Queen Elizabeth's Corgis and Princess Margaret's miniature longhaired Dachshund, Pipkin.
20. Microchip implanting of the skin.
21. A gundog which retains its working ability in the field, but can also compete in the show ring.
22. The study of canines.
23. The female parent or bitch.
24. Coursing term for a bitch.
25. The male parent or dog.
26. It was the short-legged dog used to turn the wheel of the roasting spit in the kitchen. In common use until the middle of the 19th century.
27. US (33%).
28. When a pure-bred dog's coat is of a colour not desired but still permitted in a breed standard, e.g. white, liver or blue coated German Shepherd Dogs.
29. Sight or gaze hounds; scent hounds.
30. Either the drawing of names to pair dogs for a field trial; or, in hunting terms, the action of a terrier on entering a burrow and dragging out the quarry unaided.
31. The art and science of hunting.
32. A terrier's height.
33. The head. A foreface which curves downwards from the stop to the tip of the nose, i.e. Bull Terrier.
34. Bear-baiting.
35. Irish Wolfhounds from Ireland, 1652.
36. True.
37. A silent whistle. Only the dog hears the high-pitched sounds which are beyond man's hearing limits.
38. 4027 dogs.
39. Sled dogs used to deliver the mail in winter when no other

transport can get through.

40. Hound racing popular in the Lake District and Scottish Borders. Speed race, following a drag track, with the first hound crossing the finishing line declared the winner.

41. Hounds at Hound Shows, when they are taken off the leash and exhibited free within enclosed rings.

42. 1785.

43. A Yorkshire Terrier, Summerann Thumberlina, weighing only 567grams (20oz), born on 5 January 1992.

44. Alsatian.

45. South London anti-vivisection riots in 1907, protesting against the use of a terrier in physiological experiments, in contravention of the Cruelty to Animals Act 1876.

46. Mirror Group Newspapers.

47. Sniffing out dry rot in buildings. Usually called *Rothounds*.

48. A headcollar for dog, used to prevent a dog pulling on the lead. Devised by Roger Mugford.

49. An obsolete term for a guard dog tied up during the day and released at night. Usually refered to a mastiff or mastiff-type dog.

50. St. Francis of Assisi, patron saint of animals.

51. A cross country race against the clock. Handler and dog run through a obstacle and jump course, and the handler competes on a shooting range half-way through the course.

52. Unrecognised cross-bred dog. Sighthound crossed with sheepdog or terrier.

53. An odd dog at a Field Trial which has no paired partner or brace mate.

54. When moulting or shedding hair.

55. Red.

56. c. 3.72m (12ft 2.5in)

57. 203

58. 78

59. Ch. U'Kwong King Solomon (1968-78). A Chow Chow, owned andbred by Joan Egerton.

60. 23 (American Foxhound, 1944; St Bernard, 1975; Great Dane, 1987)

61. A pair of US custom drug sniffing dogs. The Belgian Shepherds, Rocky and Barco are so successful that Mexican

drug smugglers placed a price on their heads.

62. A 5 peseta coin.
63. Heath Dog Violet. A low perennial plant with heart-shaped flowers found on heaths, open woods and fenland.
64. A Whippet.
65. Mastiff.
66. 4.
67. A cure for dog bites.
68. The gatherers ears were stopped, and a dog was tied to the plant's stem, pulling up the whole plant and root.
69. Because its thorns resemble a dog's canine teeth.
70. Poisonous to dogs.
71. 29 years (and 5 months).
72. A Greyhound called Low Pressure, also known as Timmy,. fathered more than 3000 puppies during the period December 1961 to November 1969.
73. The British classification of dogs is divided into 2 divisions – sporting and non-sporting, which are further divided into 6 groups. The Sporting Division is made up of 3 groups – Hounds, Gundogs and Terriers.The American Sporting Group is 1 of 7 Groups, and consists of bird or gundogs i.e. Pointers, Retrievers, Setters and Spaniels.
74. *Did not finish*, as used in sled dog racing and greyhound racing, meaning a racer did not finish the race.
75. A left turn.
76. Travois.
77. 1969.
78. Watchdogs.
79. Greyhound.
80. Approx. 7538 BC.
81. When one dog forces another to do most of the work while saving strength and ground, but winning most of the points in the competition.
82. Boxer.
83. Dingo, Border Collie, and Australian Terrier.
84. Chespeake Bay Retriever
85. A hound called Cavall.
86. True.
87. Chips.

88. Dominican Friars.
89. 2.
90. True
91. Domestic animal.
92. 30 barks per minute
93. 1835.
94. 1901.
95. An unspayed bitch.
96. Community or state legislation requiring dogs to be on leashes or muzzled on the street, or kept at home during prescribed curfew hours.
97. a. Centenary of the National Canine Defence League (NCDL)
     b. George Stubbs
     c. 1978
98. Tattooing, silicon microchip implants & nose prints.
99. a. A Truffle dog, a dog used to hunt for and root out truffles.
     b. Subterranean fungus, highly valued in cookery, generally growing under oak trees.
     c. Pigs or dogs. Dogs are preferred, as pigs like truffles and eat them.
100. a. The Dickin Medal.
     b. People's Dispensary for Sick Animals (PDSA).
     c. 18 dogs.
101. a. Pattern of woven or printed 4-pointed star check (resembling a dog's canine tooth), in a broken twill weave.
     b. Boucle fabric resembling the coat of a poodle.
     c. A rough crepe fabric made of twisted yarns woven to imitate tree bark, and nothing to do with dogs!
102. a. Germany.
     b. German for "protection dog".
     c. Type of advanced obedience and working dog training, which includes protection work.
103. Lewd behaviour, vomiting techniques, and embarassing habits.
104. a. The lowest throw of the dice.
     b. Cheated.
     c. You had gone to ruin.

105. a. Bad Latin.
    b. Bad verse.
    c. The letter R, also known as the "growling letter".

106. a. A scrap, or a quick, confused fight.
    b. Both fighters or wrestlers hit the ground together.
    c. The literal meaning is to lie still and silent, but also slang for staying quiet and out of sight.

107. a. A bitch pack of hounds.
    b. Beagles.
    c. A male hare.

108. a. Cure for a rabid dog bite.
    b. Ancient Romans swallowed the singed dog hair as a hangover cure.
    c. Scotch whiskey (1oz), double cream (1.25oz) & honey (0.5oz). Mix well and serve with ice.

109. a. Chicken.
    b. Cornmeal spoon bread.
    c. Rolled currant dumpling or jam pudding.

110. a. A staircase which goes back and forward without a stair-well.
    b. A 2-wheeled horse-drawn driving-cart with cross seats back to back.
    c. Parhelion, or mock sun – a spot on the solar halo at which light is intensified.

Breed Answers

111. Old English Sheepdog.
112. Bergamasco.
113. Harlequin Great Dane.
114. Boston Terriers.
115. Finnish Spitz (Suomenpystykorva).
116. Dalmatian.
117. Bedlington Terrier.
118. Airedale Terrier.
119. Whippet.
120. Poodle.
121. Brittany.
122. Basset Fauves de Bretagne.
123. Hungarian Puli.
124. Chihuahua.
125. Maltese.
126. Schipperke.
127. Pekingese.
128. Saluki.
129. German Shepherd Dog.
130. Mastiff group.
131. Dandie Dinmont Terrier.
132. Miniature Pinscher.
133. Born white, and the spots develop at about 10-14 days old.
134. White. (Sometimes has biscuit or cream markings).
135. Old English Sheepdog.
136. Papillon or Continental Toy Spaniel.
137. As tightly curled as possible.on the hip. Double curl preferred.
138. Isabella (fawn).
139. Grand Bleu de Gascogne.
140. False.
141. Great Dane.
142. No. The Basenji yodels.
143. New Guinea Singing Dog.
144. Coton de Tulear.
145. Lhasa Apso.

146. Chihuahua.
147. Bullmastiff.
148. Gordon Setter.
149. Gordon Setter.
150. Havanese or Bichon Havanese.
151. Irish Wolfhound.
152. Weimaraner.
153. A small Greyhound bred by King Frederick of Prussia, at his Potsdam palace.
154. Black and Tan Terrier.
155. A miniature Beagle, being less than 10 inches in height compared to the normal 13-16 inches.
156. English Toy Spaniels.
157. Alaskan Malamute.
158. Bloodhound.
159. Pomeranian.
160. Porcelaine Hounds.
161. Canaan Dog.
162. Rottweiler.
163. Yorkshire Terrier.
164. Briard, from Brie.
165. Belgian Shepherd Dog - the Groenendael.
166. The Hairless is hairless, except for soft hair on head, toes and tail. Powderpuff covered with long soft hair over body.
167. Arabian greyhound.
168. Morocco.
169. Swiss scenthounds.
170. Tosa Inu.
171. Pug.
172. Cardigan Welsh Corgi is larger and has a long foxbrush-type tail. Pembroke is smaller and has a short tail.
173. Bouvier de Flandres.
174. Rothbury Terrier.
175. Egyptian sheepdog.
176. Affenpinscher.
177. Used to nip at the heels of cattle to control them.
178. Japanese Akita.

179. Clumber Spaniel.
180. Term used to describe the medium-sized French hounds.
181. True.
182. Welsh Terrier.
183. Finnish Spitz.
184. Dobermann and Bergamsco.
185. Australian Cattle Dogs.
186. Pug.
187. Lhasa Apso.
188. Petit Basset Griffon Vendeen.
189. True.
190. Clumber Spaniel.
191. Chesapeake Bay Retriever.
192. Irish Terrier.
193. Norwich Terrier.
194. Bloodhound.
195. Turkey.
196. Borzoi.
197. Shar-Pei.
198. Keeshond.
199. Sleeve Pekingese.
200. Landseer (Newfoundland).
201. Greyhound.
202. Toy Spaniel (King Charles and Cavalier King Charles Spaniels).
203. Greyhound and Irish Wolfhound crosses, developed in Australia in the nineteenth century to hunt kangeroo.
204. Welsh Foxhound.
205. 2- smooth-coated and wire-haired.
206. No, they are separate breeds.
207. Irish Setter.
208. No, either a Labrador Retriever (yellow), or a Golden Retrieve.
209. Australia.
210. Smooth-coated Chow Chow.

Section 2

211. Bichon Frisé.

212. True.
213. Large, flat and round, with no arch – like a snowshoe. Heavily furnished with hair. Thick strong pads.
214. Airedale Terrier.
215. Chesapeake Bay Retriever.
216. Rolling, lose-jointed, shuffling and side-wise motion. Does not raise his feet very high off the ground.
217. Almond shaped and moderately deep set.
218. False. Does not have an undercoat.
219. True. Coat lightens with age.
220. Leonberger.
221. Yorkshire Terrier.
222. Webbed feet, designed for swimming.
223. Harrier.
224. Miniature Pinschers and Affenpinschers.
225. Giant Schnauzer.
226. Catahoula Leopard Dog.
227. English Setter. Ticking or roan coat colour patterns.
228. Only when the coat surrounding the eye is white.
229. It measures a Welsh yard (from the tip of its nose to the end of the outstretched tail).
230. West Highland White Terrier.
231. The black colour can appear weathered or rusty. The colour fades in the sun, and lacks intensity.
232. Weight.
233. Irish Water Spaniel.
234. Alert, kind, indicating a high-degree of intelligence.
235. The padding, or exceptional thickness of the upper lips or flews.
236. Scottish Deerhound.
237. Keeshond.
238. Finnish Spitz.
239. Mexican Hairless.
240. No. Introduced in Britain in 1947.
241. Kerry Blue Terrier.
242. Kuvacz is larger (88-114lbs, 40-52kg) than the

Maremma (77-99lbs, 35-45kg).

243. Shar Pei.
244. Italian Spinone.
245. Unshaven ring of hair on the hindquarters of the Poodle in the continental clip.
246. Curly Coated Retriever.
247. True.
248. Black or liver (a few white hairs permissible).
249. American Staffordshire Bull Terrier.
250. Boston Terrier.
251. 4 (Irish Terrier, Glen of Imaal Terrier, Soft Coated Wheaten Terrier, and Kerry Blue Terrier).
252. False. Red and white only.
253. Labrador Retriever.
254. Black.
255. Australian Kelpie.
256. Mexican Hairless Dog.
257. Malinois.
258. White Bull Terrier.
259. Co. Wicklow, Eire.
260. True.
261. French Bulldog.
262. German Shepherd Dogs.
263. Norwegian Lundehund (Puffin Dog).
264. Dandie Dinmont and Skye Terriers.
265. Briard.
266. 45 degree angle forward & downward to the shoulder joints.
267. Chinook.
268. Papillon has large upright butterfly, prick ears, and the Phalene has drop-ears.
269. Czesky or Bohemian Terrier.
270. True.
271. Portugal.
272. Basset Hound.
273. Beauceron, or Berger de Beauce.
274. Stripping comb or hand-stripping the coat, and plucking out the dead hair. Scissors only used to trim the eyebrows, leg hair and around the feet.
275. Results in a break down or weakness in the pasterns, which

have a greater than desirable slope away from the perpendicular when viewed side on. In practical terms, reduces the dog's efficiency in running, and the amount of exercise it is capable of taking.

276. Standard Schnauzer.
277. Chesapeake Bay Retrievers.
278. A Pug raised the alarm of the approach of the Spanish enemy at Hermingny in 1572, thereby saving the life of the William I, Prince of Orange.
279. The lozenge mark on the head of the Blenheim Cavalier King Charles Spaniel. Sometimes also used to refer to cheek marking on toy dogs in general.
280. Maltese dog.
281. False. The hindfeet are larger.
282. A generic term for shepherd dog, generally used for the Pyrenean Mountain Dog.
283. Schillerstovare or Schiller Hound.
284. In young puppies.
285. Tibetan Mastiff.
286. German Shepherd Dog.
287. False. The Beardie has a double coat which is shaggy but not so long as to hide the natural lines of the body. The coat must never be trimmed.
288. A French hound, named after the Chateau de Billy in Poitou.
289. 1945.
290. Australian Cattle Dog.
291. The jabot (also called the apron, and is the long hair between the front legs..
292. True, 1650.
293. Sredni – the medium sized Lowland Sheepdog.
294. Field Spaniels of 25lbs or under. (Also shown as Springer Spaniels).
295. St Bernard breed standard.
296. The short-haired saddle area, which is darker than that of the long coat.
297. Lakeland Terrier (Stingray of Derrybach).
298. English Springer Spaniel.
299. Strong, slightly crooked front legs which allow him, when

digging to throw out the earth to each side of him, and so not block his own progress.

300. 1860.
301. Swedish Vallhund (Vasgotaspets).
302. Guard and defence dogs against the native Indians.
303. Sealyham Terrier.
304. Great Britain.
305. Black and Tan Coonhound.
306. Any mixed-breed hound that has solid tan markings.
307. Foxhound.
308. Shar-Pei.
309. Wirehaired Pointing Griffon.

Section 3

310. Australian Silky Terrier. The Silky is in the Toy Group, the others are in the Terrier Group.
311. Shiba Inu. It is a Japanese breed, the others are Chinese.
312. Saluki. It originates in the Middle East, the others are both African breeds.
313. Welsh Corgi. It has a short-medium length coat. The others come in 2 different coat-types – rough and smooth.
314. Anatolian Shepherd Dog. It is a flock guarding breed, the others are herding and shepherding breeds.
315. Harrier. It is a scent hound, the others are sight hounds.
316. Rottweiler. It is a shortcoated breed, the others are long-haired, with stand-off coat.
317. Tibetan Mastiff. The others have blue-black tongues.
318. Basset Hound. It has a sabre-tail, the others have curled tails set on high.
319. Whippet. It has rose ears, the others have prick or erect ears.
320. Dandie Dinmont Terrier. It has a long, low body, the others have cobby, compact bodies.
321. Irish Water Spaniel. It is an Irish water dog, the others are English land gundogs.
322. Norwich Terrier. It is a short-legged terrier, the others are long-legged terriers.
323. Groenendael. It has a black coat, the others are born with black/dark coats which lighten as the dog matures.

324. Italian Greyhound. It is a smooth-coated toy breed, the others are members of the longer coated Bichon family

Section 4

325. Basenji.
326. Bull Terrier.
327. Kerry Blue Terrier.
328. Norfolk Terrier.
329. Saluki.
330. Saluki.
331. Saluki.
332. Irish Setter and Irish Wolfhound.
333. Cocker Spaniel.
334. Irish Setter.
335. Labrador Retriever.
336. Labrador Retriever.
337. Gordon Setter.
338. Schnauzers.
339. Pointer.
340. Pyrenean Mountain Dog.
341. Boxer
342. Great Dane
343. Deerhound.
344. Scottish Terrier.
345. Boxer.
346. Bulldog and Border Terrier.
347. Border Terrier.
348. Poodle.
349. Irish Water Spaniel.
350. Smooth Fox Terrier.
351. Samoyed.
352. Miniature Dachshund.
353. Poodle.
354. Irish Red & White Setter.
355. Border Terrier.
356. Kerry Blue Terrier.
357. Golden Retriever.
358. Basenji.
359. French Bulldog.

360. Borzoi.
361. Griffon Bruxellois.
362. Cairn Terrier.
363. Whippet.
364. Airedale Terrier.
365. Golden Retriever.
366. West Highland White Terrier.
367. Bloodhound.
368. Field Spaniel.
369. Cocker Spaniel.
370. German Spitz.
371. Hungarian Vizsla.
372. Airedale Terrier.
373. Golden Retriever.
374. Cardigan Welsh Corgi.

Section 5

375. a. A ridge of hair on the back, growing in the opposite direction to the rest of the coat.
   b. Phu-Quoc Dog, or the Mha Kon Klab.
   c. Thailand.

376. a. Haldenstovare.
   b. Scent hound.
   c. Schillerstovare, Hamiltonstovare, & Smalandsstovare.

377. a. Brabancon.
   b. Pug.
   c. Griffon d'Ecurie, or stable Griffon.

378. Smooths – Petit Brabancon.
   Rough Reds – Brussels Griffons.
   Rough other colours – Belgian Griffons.

379. a. Dachshunds.
   b. Teckel.
   c. By chest circumference.

Breed Answers

380. a.   1st premolars.
    b.   Class 1 Certificate for Breeding.
c.   3 or more missing teeth.

381. a.   Groenendael.
    b.   Laekenois.
    2c.   Malinois.

382. a.   1913.
    b.   Cream.
    c.   US and Canada.

383. a.   Shetland Sheepdog.
    b.   Colloquial for farmdog, from the Gaelic "Toon" meaning farm.
    c.   1906.

384. The Vendeen.   Grand Griffon-Vendeen
                  Briquet Griffen Vendeen
                  Grand Basset Griffon Vendeen
                  Petit Basset Griffon Vendeen.

385. a.   Black with tan markings; ruby; and red and white.
    b.   Tri-colour.
    c.   Prince Charles.

386. a.   Norfolk has drop-ears, the Norwich has prick-ears.
    b.   1964.
    c.   1979.

387. a.   Alaskan Malamute.
    b.   Eskimo Dog.
    c.   Siberian Husky.

388. a.   Fila Brasileiro.
    b.   Dogue de Bordeaux.
    c.   Mastiff.

389. a.   Little Lion Dog, or Petit Chien Lion.

b.   Lion cut, front half of body left long to resemble a lion's mane, back half and tail clipped,leaving only a plume at the end of the tail.

c.   Long, soft and silky. Can be any colour.

390. a.   Maltese.
b.   Chihuahua.
c.   Pharoah Hound.

391. a.   Coursing wolves.
b.   Matched for size and speed, but also matched for coat colour and markings.

392. a.   Pointer.
b.   Setter.
c.   Starters.

393. a.   After the game is shot, the dog is sent out to pick up and retrieve.
b.   Works in the open, finding and holding the game, but not retrieving. Scents the air for birds and then stays still and silent "pointing" to and holding the game.
c.   Works in cover and undergrowth, finding, flushing out and retrieving game.

394. a.   5 varieties.
b.   Standard (Mittel) German Spitz; Small (Klein) German Spitz.
c.   Keeshond.

395. a.   Jack Russell/Parson Jack Russell Terrier.
b.   Hunting terrier developed to drive foxes from their underground lairs.
c.   The longer-legged Parson Jack Russell, standing 14in at the shoulder.

396 a.   Retrieved lost nets and tackle.
b.   Courier between fishing boats .
c.   Guard-dog for the boat, tackle and "catch" when ashore.

397. a.   Boxer.
     b.   Boxer.
     c.   Flock St Salvator.

398. a.   Irish Red and White Setter.
     b.   Irish Red and White is shorter, wider and sturdier; has
     higher set ear; has less heavy feathering; its skull is domed
     without occipital protuberance as in the Irish Setter.

399. a.   All colours.
     b.   Red, small white marking allowed.
     c.   Black or liver.

Section 6

400. Schipperke.
401. French Bulldog.
402. Yorkshire Terrier.
403. Norfolk Terrier.
404. Chihuahua.
405. Chinese Crested.
406. Bedlington Terrier.
407. Manchester Terrier.
408. Chow Chow.
409. Keeshond.
410. Collie (Rough).
411. Pug.
412. Skye Terrier.
413. St Bernard.
414. Brussels Griffon (Griffon Bruxellois).
415. Afghan Hound.
416. Sussex Spaniel.
417. Saluki.
418. Tibetan Terrier.
419. Bloodhound.
420. Pointer.
421. Maltese.
422. Greyhound.
423. Curly-coated Retriever.

Veterinary Answers

425. Free from major faults, using the relevant breed standard as a guide.
426. Characteristics or distinguishing features required by a dog, based on the requirements of the breed standard.
427. Overall appearance and bone structure of the dog.
428. Angles created by the bones at the joints, particularly at the shoulder, stifle, hock, the pasterns and the pelvic area.
429. Has the correct range of angulation for a given breed.
430. Horses.
431. A dog's upper outline from the withers or shoulder to the base of the tail, as seen in profile.
432. Approximately 320 bones.
433. The skin.
434. 13 pairs.
435. 16, 4 per foot.
436. 3 phalanges per toe.
437. Approx. 70%.
438. Femur, or thigh bone.
439. Achilles tendon.
440. 13th rib, which remains completely unattached ventrally. Allows greater lung expansion in the chest cavity.
441. Breastbone (sternum). Also used to describe the chest or thorax.
442. The knee joint.
443. 5 – large middle and 4 digital pads.
444. Stopper pad. Protective covering around the accessory bone.
445. Bones and joints.
446. 38.5 degrees centigrade (101.5F).
447. No. Higher, 39 degrees centigrade (102F).
448. 90-100 beats per minute.
449. True.
450. 20 upper teeth, 22 lower teeth.
451. 28.
452. Close family breeding, i.e. brother to sister, father to daughter, son to mother.
453. Sense of touch.

454. A shortage of or imbalance of calcium and phosphorus.
455. Gregor Mendel.
456. Artificial insemination.
457. Father (sire).
458. Average 63 days (9 weeks). Pregnancies lasting between 55-71 days are considered normal.
459. 10.
460. A dog's shape, size, colour, sex, temperament, state of health and intelligence.
461. A feature or defect which is present a birth.
462. A male dog in which both testicles are seen to be present in the scrotum. Unspayed bitches are also sometimes called "entire".
463. Neutering.
464. Progressive Retinal Atrophy.
465. Affects the eyes, leading to blindness.
466. Hard Pad Disease. Nose and pads often become thickened, cracked and dry.
467. The ear. It is the inflamation of the external ear canal.
468. Viral disease.
469. Ticks.
470. To prevent a injured dog hurting itself, by biting, pulling at stiches, chewing or tearing at a plaster cast or bandages.
471. The inside of the thigh – the artery just under the skin.
472. Yes.
473. To prevent bacterial placque and tartar from forming at the base of the teeth and gums. If the placque and tartar are not removed, the gums can become infected, may recede, and the dog gets bad breath.
474. Proteins, carbohydrates, fats, vitamins and minerals.
475. To avoid draughts.
476. Keeping a dog's teeth and gums healthy.
477. Chicken, game or fish boñes. These may lodge in the throat, or puncture the intestines.
478. Dog's sense of smell.
479. Minor bleeding: keeping direct pressure on the wound until bleeding stops and /or applying an ice pack. Severe bleeding: applying a tourniquet.
480. True.

481. Yes
482. A malformation of the hip joint, where the socket (acetabulum) is too shallow and/or the head of the femur (the ball) is too flat and irregular in shape. The poorly formed joint is susceptible to wear and tear leading to pain, difficulty in walking and arthritis.
483. The outer coat's guard hairs on the neck and the back are raised. This is involuntary and is caused by fear and anger. Used to impress or scare off the enemy.
484. Cutting the nail too short, and cutting through the quick, which contains the blood vessels and nerves. This is painful, and the cut may bleed freely for a short time.
485. Having well developed, strong muscles, i.e. top physical condition.
486. Overdeveloped in the shoulder blades.
487. Pasterns.
488. Canine parvovirus.
489. True.
490. Increases the length of stride.
491. Sight or gaze hounds.
492. Greyhound, which can run at 40mph over short distances.
493. 20.
494. Through their pads, mouth and tongue, but not through the skin
495. Remnants of the thumb located on the forefeet. Located on the inner surface of the pasterns on the hindfeet.
496. Keep the coat clean; prevent matting of the hair, and remove any loose hair, dust or dirt; stimulate the circulation.
497. A corded coat.
498. 2 coats. Soft undercoat for warmth, with harsher, weatherproof outercoat.
499. Coat is made up of a mass of tight curls, which trap the air and protect the dog from water and the cold.
500. Airborne infection, spread from the infected mucous or airborne droplets from a coughing dog.
501. The body's shock absorbers. Located at the junction where the paw meets the foreleg.
502. The locking together of the dog and the bitch during mating, caused by the swelling of the bulbis glandis just behind the penis.

503. Part of the bitch's milk which provides the puppies with immunity from disease.
504. Flesh-coloured, light or brown nose. Usually a breed fault, but is required by some breeds, such as the Brittany or the Pharaoh Hound.
505. The leather.
506. The bridge of the nose.
507. White and blue eyes, usually associated with merle coat colour.
508. A round eye which protrudes slightly.
509. Pads which are thin and lack cushioning.
510. Toes which point inwards.
511. Specialised feet of the Arctic breeds, adapted for rough icy terrain. Oval, firm and compact, with well-knitted, well-arched toes, and deeply cushioned pads. Webbed between the toes and well furred.
512. True.
513. Alaskan Malamute and Siberian Husky.
514. a. Rickets, poor teeth, poor muscle tone, failure to assimilate calcium and phosphorous.

   b. Failure to grow, anaemia, liver disorder.

   c. Rickets, bone malformations, hyper-irritability of nerves and muscles.
515. The Loin, from the end of the ribcage to the start of the pelvis.

Rules Answers

Section 1

516. 7.
517. A dog born in the US, as a result of a mating which also occurred in the US.
518. 6 months from the date of whelping. Late registration (6-12 months) will be considered if full information provided and penalty fee paid.
519. No individual puppies can be registered unless the litter was first registered by the owner or leasee of the dam at the time of whelping.
520. No litters to be registered from a dam that is less than 8 months old or over 12 years old, at the time of mating.
521. No litters to be registered sired by a dog under 7 months or over 12 years old, at the time of mating.
522. No.
523. 5 years (renewable for further 5 years).
524. Making continuous use of the kennel name. If not continuously used for a period of more than 6 years, the AKC will regard the kennel name has having been abandoned.
525. No.
526. Whether there is sufficient national interest in the new breed, and whether there is a sufficient gene pool in both numbers and diversity – usually 300-400 dogs nationally.
527. No. The AKC will only consider applications from clubs and societies, who are required to have maintained suitable and accurate pedigree/breeding records for the several generations of US-born dogs which have bred true.
528. No. Litters born outside of the US must be registered with the appropriate national kennel club.
529. An interim stage prior to a breed being eligible to compete in a variety group at AKC shows. When a new breed is eligible for registration, the breed will be placed in the Miscellaneous Class for a specified time while deciding which variety group it will join.

530. Normally varies from 1-3 years before moving into a specific Variety Group.

531. Obedience and tracking events, matches, and miscellaneous classes.

532. At least 5 years after the dog has died.

533. Colour and markings.

534. AKC Investigations and Inspections Department.

535. Deals with foreign and limited registrations. Coonhound registrations are handled by the AKC/ACHA Coonhound Department which deals with registrations, pedigrees, hunt and bench show dates and results, and championship titles.

536. Show at which Championship points may be awarded, given by a club or association which is a member of the AKC.

537. A show at which championship points may be awarded, given by a club or association which is not a member of the AKC, but has obtained an AKC license to hold a specific show.

538. A show restricted to the breeds and varieties in any one group, at which championship points may be awarded.

539. A show given by a single breed club or association, at which championship points may be awarded.

540. A show restricted to American-bred dogs held by a single breed club or association, at which championship points may be awarded.

541. Informal meeting at which pure-bred dogs may compete, but no championship points are awarded. Meeting may be held by variety of clubs, but need the sanction of the AKC.

542. Member clubs and associations can hold 1 show and 1 field trial without payment of a fee to the AKC. Any additional fees or trials can be held upon payment of a fee to the AKC. Non-member clubs and associations must apply to the AKC for permission to hold specific shows, and pay the relevant fee.

543. When the Member club or association fails to hold a show at least once in 2 consecutive years. The AKC then has the right to grant another club or association permission to hold a show within the limits of the show territory of the original club or association.

544. 6 months, except at sanctioned matches when approved by the AKC.
545. Champions.
546. Class for dogs 6 months or over, born in the US, Canada, Mexico or Bermuda, which have not, prior to the date of closing of entries, won 3 First Prizes in the novice class, a 1st prize in Bred-by-Exhibitor, American-bred, or Open classes, nor one or more points towards their Championships.
547. Class for any dog 6 months or over, except in a Member Speciality Club Show held only for American-bred dogs, in which case Open Classes will be for American-bred dogs only.
548. Class divided by sex, each division only open to undefeated dogs of the same sex which have won 1st prizes in either Puppy, Twelve-to-Eighteen Month, Novice, Bred-by-Exhibitor, American-Bred, or open Classes. After Winners Prize awarded, the 2nd prize winning dogs, if undefeated except by the dog awarded Winners, shall compete with other eligible dogs for Reserve Winners. No eligible dog may be withheld from competition. Winners Class shall be allowed at shows where American-Bred and Open Classes shall be given. Winners receive the points at the show.
549. No.
550. Best of Breed, or Best of Variety.
551. 15 points, which entitles the dog to have "Ch." used before its name.
552. A dog can earn from 1 – 5 points at a show.
553. Points are awarded on the number of dogs in the actual competition, with more points being awarded for larger classes. AKC compile an annual schedule which will determine the number of points required for different breeds, sex, and geographical location.
554. The 15 points must be won under at least 3 different judges, and must include 2 "majors" (wins of 3-5 points) won under 2 different judges.
555. To obtain an Obedience title. A "leg" being an obedience test score of at least 170 out of a maximum 200 points, and a score of more than 50% on each exercise.

556. Novice, Open, and Utility.
557. Tests, held under AKC regulations, which require a dog to follow a trail by scent.
558. TDX stands for Tracking Dog Excellent, an award given for success in the advanced tests.
559. Yes.
560. Title given to a dog that has successfully completed the highest level of the 3 Hunting Tests.
561. Testing and Trial sections.
562. An award given to a dog which shows an inherent herding ability and is trainable in herding.
563. An award given to a dog which has basic herding training, and can herd a small group of livestock through a simple course.
564. 15 Championship points.

Section 2

565. Full and Associate members.
566. a.   Full.
    b.   Full.
    c.   Full.
    d.   Full.
    e.   Associate.
    f.   Associate.
    g.   Full.
    h.   Full.

567. Each full member sends 3 delegates who together have only 1 vote.
568. 4 years, but can be re-elected.
569. Twice a year.
570. Europe, America, Asia, Africa, Oceania and Australia.
571. President, Vice-President, and Treasurer.
572. Legal, Scientific, and Standards Commissions.
573. English, French, German and Spanish.
574. A list of their national breeds, and corresponding breed standards, which must be set out according to the model adopted by the FCI.

575. The General Assembly. Modifications and new provisional standards are approved by the General Committee
576. The Standards Commission, and if a new breed is to be admitted the advice of the Scientific Commission must be sought.
577. Simultaneously in the 4 official languages.
578. Yes.
579. Yes, but those granted by its affiliated organisations.
580. Yes.
581. All-Breeds and International Trials at which the FCI awards international championship certificates.
582. The governing national bodies retain responsibility for their own judges, but they must be recognized by the FCI.
583. A list of recognised judges with a list of the breeds or groups which they are entitled to judge.
584. 10 Groups.
585. Championship Aptitude Certificate of International Beauty.
586. International Dog-Show with attribution of the FCI CACIB.
587. Minimum of 4, with an extra one granted for every additional 5,000 dogs registered in the national Stud Book.
588. Only 1 can be awarded on the same day and at the same place.
589. Open, working and Champion Classes.
590. Title of International Champion of Beauty of the FCI, or a title of National Champion in a country affiliated to the FCI.
591. 15 months.
592. A dog drawing very close to the ideal breed standard, and which is in perfect condition. It should also have the characteristics of its sex.
593. A dog which is sufficiently typed without notable qualities, or not in very good physical condition.
594. Open, working or Championship Classes, to the exclusion of other classes.
595. No.
596. Yes, if invited.
597. 4 CACIBS in 3 different countries, given by 3 different judges, whatever the number of competitors. One CACIB must be obtained in the owner's country of residence, or the country of origin of the breed.
598. 25 years old.

599. Breed knowledge, and ring procedure.
600. Breed, Group and All Round Judge.
601. Up to 80 dogs per day.
602. Up to 150 dogs per day.
603. Agility European Championships.
604. Maximum of 8 dogs.
605. Personal record of a dog's competition scores, which is compulsory for FCI competitions.
606. Field Trials.
607. Decision that CACIT should be awarded solely at trials organized on live game, and the trials should have the character of practical hunting, organized on natural game.
608. Field Trials for Retriever Breed Dogs.
609. Partridge.
610. Minimum of 2 and maximum of 4.
611. Odedience and defence, and tracking.
612. 3. International Competition Classes 1-3.
613. Mediocre.

Section 3

614. Championship Show, Open Show and Open Parade.
615. Yes.
616. Exhibition of registered dogs, at which Champion dogs may not compete, and at which no Challenge Certificate points are awarded. Regarded as the training ground for new exhibitors.
617. Championship Show.
618. Informal gathering by a non-affiliated club or society, which has asked permission from canine governing authority to hold a sanctioned event.
619. For dogs of 3 months and under 6 months of age.
620. For dogs over 18 and not over 36 months of age.
621. For dogs 6 months of age or over which have not won a 1st prize at any Open Parade or Championship Show.
622. For dogs 6 months or older whelped in the State in which it is exhibited.
623. For dogs 6 months or older whelped in Australia.
624. For all dogs of 6 months or over. May be confined to

specific breed or variety at Championship or Breed Shows.

625. 7.
626. 4.
627. A dog can only have the highest Obedience title after its name.
628. No Novice only for dogs of any breed, 6 months or over, which are not eligible for the title of Companion Dog (CD).
629. Companion Dog Excellent, a certificate obtained through receiving 3 scores of 170 points or more in Utility Classes.
630. Minimum 3 and maxiumum of 10.
631. No, unless specifically requested, dogs are generally given the opportunity to complete the Trial exercises.
632. Utility Dog Class.
633. Minimum length must be 750mm.
634. "Heel on lead", and "Stand for Examination".
635. Enters and leaves on the lead.
636. 3 different varieties.
637. If the handler continuously tugs at the lead.
     If the handler adapts his pace to the dog.
     If the dog does not complete the principle feature of the exercise.
638. 200 points
639. A dog must have a Companion Dog (CD) title, and have passed the Preliminary Tracking qualification title.
640. Must successfully complete Test 1 & 2, tracking 1 known person and one unknown person.
641. A person (known to the handler or unknown depending on the test) who places articles on the track at places nominated by the judge, and places an additional article at the start of each track. The tracklayer follows the track marked out earlier collecting all the flags along the way. At the end of each track, he remains silent and still, waiting to be found.
642. 18 months of age.
643. 4 dogs, and 4 different owners.
644. 3, with a least 2 different judges.
645. Finishing in the top half of the number of dogs competing in the 2nd round of a trial, or having completed a faultless round in either the 1st or 2nd round at the same trial. Only 1

qualifiying card gained at a Specialist Breed Agility Trial will be accepted.

646. 450mm.
647. Maxmimum number of 30.
648. No.
649. A bonus 5 second deduction from the final time for a specific round.
650. 5 seconds added to the course time for each mistake or fault.
651. "Are you ready"?
652. Penalty for misbehaviour.
653. Brittany, German Shorthaired Pointer, German Wirehaired Pointer, Large Munsterlander, Hungarian Vizsla, and the Weimaraner.
654. Yes.
655. To seek and retrieve fallen game, when ordered to do so. He should sit quietly with the handler, or anywhere where the handler was directed him to, until ordered to retrieve.
656. 12 points in Non-Retrieving trials. Gained by winning outright a Championship Stake or National Championships, or by winning outright 2 All Age Stakes, or by being placed 2nd in 2 Championship Stakes or National Championships, or winning outright 1 All Age Stake and being placed 2nd in a Championship Stake or National Championships.
657. Quail.
658. Minimum of 6 runners, belonging to at least 4 different owners.
659. No.
660. Only 1.
661. A discretionary award given by the judge if a dog has shown that it is not gun-shy, and that it will hunt, point and back naturally.
662. Double rise, the 2nd object of game being thrown while the dog is returning with the first.

Section 4

663. 6 groups.
664. 3 – Hounds, Gundogs and Terriers.
665. A separate register for imported dogs of new and

unregistered breeds. May be transfered to the normal breed register, at a later date, if there is sufficient interest shown in the new breed. Also includes imported dogs, which although already recognised, have had no registrations for 10 years.

666. Any type of dog, whether pure-bred or mongrel. A restrictive form of registration, with dogs limited to only Obedience and Working Trial competitions.

667. A dog's name cannot be changed after 30 days from the date at which the dog qualified for entry in the Stud Book, ie. 30 days after it won its first qualifying award.

668. The registered owner's restrictions placed on his dog's records, which may prevent the dog from taking part in shows and other licensed competitions; prevent its offspring from being registered; prevent the dog from being exported; and prevent anyone changing the dog's name.

669. No, only registered after leaving 6 month quarantine, and only if the Kennel Club has a reciprocal agreement with national canine authority from the country of origin.

670. No, a dog must be registered before it leaves the country.

671. No. A dog with cropped ears is barred from competing in any licensed event.

672. 8 years old.

673. 6 litters.

674. Hounds bred by recognised British Hunts.

675. Change of name applied for.

676. Masters of Harriers and Beagles Association.

677. Breed, General, Dog Training, Agility and Ringcraft Societies.

678. Large agricultural or municipal societies or associations, which wish to include a licensed dog show, as part of a much larger agricultural or civic event.

679. A national list of recognised ringcraft societies.

680. A Council made up of representatives of registered breed societies, which provide specialist knowledge and advice on their breed. Can make representations to the General Committe of the Kennel Club regarding the breed standard, and on applications to register new breed societies.

681. 1 licensed show per year.

682. Annually, every Jaanuary.
683. 7.
684. Sanction, Primary, Exemption Shows, and Matches.
685. Show at which registered and unregistered dogs can compete. May be held by an unregistered society, which applied to the Kennel Club for permission to hold it.
686. Show which is restricted to members of a Show Society, providing up to 10 classes if a single breed show, or up to 25 classes if more than 1 breed to be exhibited.
687. Must not be less than 500 sq feet of floor space.
688. Minimum of 4 awards.
689. 6 months old.
690. Yes.
691. At shows featuring more than 1 breed.
692. If won in a breed class for which no Challenge Certificate was on offer.
693. 5 or more point green stars.
694. A gundog or Collie dog that has won 3 Challenge Certificates, under 3 different judges, with one Challenge Certificate being given when the dog is over 12 months of age.
695. A dog which is 7 years old or above, which can compete in the Veteran Classes.
696. 3 or more belonging to 1 exhibitor. The dogs must be individually entered into classes apart from team or brace.
697. Obedience shows.
698. Agility Tests.
699. A walk plank (4'6" high x 12-14' long, and 10-12" wide) with fixed ramps on each end. Last 3ft of each ramp painted a different colour to show where the dog must land.
700. 18 months, except Bloodhounds who can compete when 12 months old.
701. Patrol Dog (PD) and Tracking Dog (TD) Stakes.
702. No.
703. A Club or inter-Club competition, but only amongst registered clubs and societies.
704. When the dog is seen to approach and unhesitatingly pick out a runner from a group of 3 at the end of the line.
705. Only if the dog has gained both sections of the Working

Permit issued by the Association of Bloodhound Breeders or the Bloodhound Club, which certifies that they are steady with farm animals.

706. Retrievers and Irish Water Spaniels.
     Sporting Spaniels other than Irish Water Spaniels.
     Pointers and Setters.
     Hunt, Point and Retrieve breeds.

707. A Warrant issued to a dog that has won 25 points between the ages of 12 to 18 months old. The scale of points varies but includes 3 points for first prizes in a breed class at a Championship Show where Challenge Certificates were on offer. Open show wins and other breed class wins only count as 1 point.

708. Postgraduate.

709. Up to 100 dogs.

710. 3 refusals or 3 run outs.

711. A breed standard of recognised breed which has not been granted Challenge Certificates.

712. A number allocated to a dog who has won a Challenge Certificate, Reserve Challenge Certificate, or a qualifying palce in the classes which are in the Band for their breed. Also dogs winning qualifying awards at Field Trials, Working Trials, and Champion Obedience Awards.

Show Answers

713. Newcastle-upon-Tyne, June 28 & 29 1859.
714. Pointers and Setters.
715. 60.
716. Birmingham, 1860.
717. The American Kennel & Sporting Field, by Arnold Burges, 1876.
718. No awards given.
719. Pointer and Setter Show, Mineola, New York, October 7th 1874.
720. The Kennel Club.
721. 1865, Southill.
722. 1874 Tennessee Sportsmen's Association combined dog show & field trial at Memphis.
723. May 8-10 1877.
724. Public demand to view the 1201 dogs entered.
725. Kentucky Derby.
726. Birmingham National (1860).
727. The Hound Show, Peterborough.
728. The Hound Show, Peterborough, 1879.
729. Scottish National Exhibition of Sporting and Other Dogs, February 20-22, 1871, Glasgow.
730. 1882.
731. Royal Melbourne Show.
732. Early pre-1859 dog shows, informal gatherings usually in pubs and taverns.
733. Early American dog shows, usually limited to members of clubs or societies, 1884-1895.
734. Westminster Dog Show because it is held in Madison Square Garden Centre, New York.
735. Manchester Championship Dog Show, the 2nd oldest continuously held dog show in the world.
736. Terriers.
737. 1891.
738. 1991 (Centenary show)....
739. The Kennel Club..
740. Stopped when the Kennel Club took over Crufts, which became the premier British dog show.

741. Cruft's Exhibition of Terriers, 1890.
742. Crufts 1915.
743. Crufts 1892. Alexandra, Princess of Wales's Pomeranian; Grand Duke Nicholas of Russia's Borzoi; and Prince Henry of Battenburg's Collie.
744. June 8th 1895, Ranelagh Club, Barn Elms.
745. Scottish Kennel Club's 40th Show, 1923.
746. Ladies' Kennel Association own Championship status, which was not recognised by the Kennel Club. LKA winners received silver/enamelled medals. On winning 3 medals, the dog held the title of LKA Champion, the wins were recorded in the LKA's own stud book and were published in the Ladies' Kennel Journal.
747. Paignton & District Fanciers Association's Show, 1930.
748. Belfast Championship Dog Show.
749. September 30 – October 2 1926. The Sesquicentennial, or Sesqui Show at Philadelphia, commemorating the nation's sesquicentenary, 1776-1926.
750. Westminster Kennel Club.
751. Ch Barberryhill Bootlegger, Sealyham Terrier.
752. 1928.
753. Primley Sceptre, Greyhound.
754. November 17-18, 1984. Centennial Dog Show & Obedience Trial, Philadephia Civic Centre.
755. Ch Cory Tucker Hills Manhattan, German Shepherd Dog.
756. Sh Ch Raycroft Socialite, Clumber Spaniel.
757. William L Kendrick.
758. Leonard Pagliero.
759. Crufts Centenary Show, 1991.
760. July 23-25 1988, Canberra, at "Australian Day" weekend.
761. Irish Kennel Club.
762. Charles Cruft.
763. Kennel Club's 70th Championship Show, October 7-8 1931.
764. Bala, Wales, 1873.
765. King's Kelpie.
766. Government House, and Canberra House, the official residence of the British High Commissioner.
767. Canberra dog shows.
768. French Bulldog Club of America.

769. West of England Ladies' Kennel Society.
770. Worcester, Herefordshire & Gloucestershire.
771. Foxhound and hunt terrier show, which is associated with the development of the Fox Terrier.
772. By weight. Large terriers over 9lbs, small terriers under 9lbs.
773. Manchester Terrier (Black and Tan Terriers).
774. Norwich Terrier......
775. Westminster Dog Show, 1928.
776. Midland Counties Canine Society (originally Leamington & County Canine Society).
777. National Invitational Championship Show, 1992.
778. April 1973.
779. 1975.
780. Leicester City Canine Society Ch. Show.
781. Prior to Blackpool 1939, all 2-day shows were run as 1 event, and all dogs had to return for the 2nd day. Blackpool obtained permission to hold the show as 2 separate day shows, allowing dogs to go home after the 1st day.
782. Crufts, Scottish Kennel Club and Welsh Kennel Club.
783. 1899.
784. Electricians strike at Olympia.
785. British epidemic of Foot and Mouth Disease.
786. General, group, and breed.
787. Crufts.
788. Houston, Texas.
789. 1900.
790. Newfoundland.
791. 1947.
792. 1970.
793. Championship stakes for all AKC registerable pointing breeds, who have won or been placed in AKC licensed or member club stakes, with at least 8, 13, or 17 starters. Gundog stake either open or amateur, or amateur/open or amateur/limited.
794. Her Majesty The Queen's estate at Sandringham, Norfolk.
795. Gordon Setters.
796. Speciale Venerie.
797. Classes for groups of 6, and full packs.

798. Total of 4, 2 each Spring and Autumn.
799. 5. 4 Nationals and 1 International.
800. 1932.
801. 1936 (Mount Kisco, New York).
802. Leonard Brumby, Snr. Memorial Trophy for Top Junior Handler, at Westminster Dog Show.
803. Mrs Challinor Ellis, judged Basset Hounds, at the 3rd Ladies' Kennel Association Show, 1897.
804. An individual qualified to judge a large number of breeds.
805. 1947.
806. Sweden and Australia.
807. R.A.S. Kennel Control, 1966.
808. Amsterdam All-Winners Dog Show.
809. Paris Dog Show.
810. Stockholm Dog Show.
811. New Zealand Kennel Club's Tux Show.
812. Berne, Switzerland.

Organisations Answers

Section 1

813. Federation Cynologique Internationale.
814. Royal Society for the Prevention of Cruelty To Animals.
815. Scottish Society for the Prevention of Cruelty to Animals.
816. Irish Society for the Prevention of Cruelty to Animals.
817. International Sheep Dog Society.
818. American Kennel Club.
819. British Veterinary Association.
820. Australian National Kennel Control.
821. New Zealand Kennel Club.
822. The Kennel Club.
823. Dog Writers' Association of America.
824. NCDL (National Canine Defence League).
825. German Shepherd Dog League and Club of GB founded in 1924. Originally called Alsatian League and Club of GB.
826. The Old English Sheepdog Club founded in 1888.
827. To hold Working Trials.
828. The Sheepdog Workers Association.
829. La Societe Royale Saint-Hubert.
830. Societe de Venerie.
831. Musee de la Venerie at Senlis; Musee Internationale de la Chasse at Gien.
832. Leeds Castle, Kent.
833. Birmingham Museum & Art Gallery.
834. Zoological Museum, Tring, Hertfordshire (now part of the Natural History Museum).
835. Dog Museum of America.
836. Soft-Coated Wheaten Terrier Club of America.
837. Pharaoh Club of England; Pharaoh Club of America, Inc.
838. American Bulldog.
839. United Kennel Club.
840. The Dutch Barge Dog Club (1925).
841. American Kennel Club.
842. American Dog Owners Association.
843. American Dog Owners Association.

844. Guide Dogs for the Blind Association. It breeds and trains all their own dogs.

845. Dogs' Home, Battersea.

846. The Retired Greyhound Trust.

847. Angell Memorial Hospital, Boston.

848. National Veterinary Medical Association.

849. A "Pets As Therapy" dog, which is taken by their owner into hospitals, old people's homes, etc. to spend time with patients and residents.

850. PRO-DOGS National Charity.

851. Belgium 1859. Belgian sheepdogs were used officially on night duty by the Ghent police.

852. Royal Navy.

853. Fund for the Replacement of Animals in Medical Experiments.

854. Trained to recognise certain sounds, and to alert their owners by touch when these sounds occur i.e. door bell, telephone ringing, and alarm clocks ringing.

855. National Beagle Club (US) established 1888. The Beagle Club formed later in 1890.

856. Siberian Husky Dog Club of GB.

857. Wolf Society of GB.

858. Swiss Alpine Club.

859. Royal Army Veterinary Corps.

860. New Zealand.

861. Singapore Kennel Club.

862. American Kennel Club.

863. Singapore Kennel Club.

864. Kennel Union of Southern Africa.

865. German Kennel Club (Verband fur das Deutsche Hundewesen).

866. South Africa.

867. Berne.

868. Oslo.

869. Ramat Gan.

870. Aubervillers.

871. Toronto.

872. Royal Agricultural Society Kennel Control, New South Wales.

873. North Australian Canine Association.
874. Australia.
875. Australia.
876. Irish Kennel Club.
877. Centenary of the Scottish Kennel Club.
878. Group established in 1953 to co-ordinate canine activities in Denmark, Finland, Norway & Sweden.
879. 1873.
880. 1884.
881. National Field Trial Club.
882. American Kennel Club.
883. 1888.
884. America.
885. 1884.
886. Independent kennel club, which has reciprocal agreements with other National kennel clubs, including Britain.
887. 1973.
888. 1964.
889. 1956.
890. 1911.
891. Thuin, Belgium.
892. 1874.
893. 1878.
894. 1925.
895. 1858.

Section 2

896. Univerity of Toronto School of Medicine, Canada.
897. Approx. 70%.
898. Royal Navy, Great Britain.
899. 1977.
900. The Master Eye Institute, founded in 1926.
901. To provide nation-wide protection for children and animals.
902. George T Ansell, who established the Massachusetts Society for the Protection of Animals.
903. The Tail-Waggers' Club & World League for Dog Welfare.
904. News of the World.

905. International Rescue Dog Organisation (IRO).
906. Events staged in Britain to promote working dogs in society.
907. Guide Dogs for the Blind Association. The theme summarising the partnership between guide dogs and their owners.
908. Joint Animal Committee, made up of a representatives of British animal charities, vet associations & local authorities.
909. Inter-Groom.
910. Scotsmen living abroad could be admitted to the Club.
911. An Afghan Hound not a Greyhound.
912. Confederation Canina Americana. An amalgamation of national kennel clubs in South America.
913. Gait: observing dogs in motion, 1974.
914. National Dog Club.
915. In 1736, freemasons were excommunicated by Pope Clement XII, some set up a new order to continue the old traditions, and the new organisation was named The Order of the Pug.
916. Commemorates the Pug as the royal dog of the House of Orange.
917. Pekingese.
918. The Blue Cross.
919. Frankfurt, Germany.
920. 16.
921. Association formed to sort out the confusion regarding the various Eastern breeds, i.e. Lhasa Apso, Shihi Tzu, Japanese Chins, etc.
922. Mastiffs. Prefix for Old English Mastiff Club.
923. Professional Handlers Association or Dog Handlers Guild.
924. Verein Fur Deutsch Schaferhunde (S.V.).
925. The Dachshund Club established in 1881, the Deutsch Teckelklub established in 1888.
926. Association formed in 1873 in Russia to protect and promote the older type of Borzoi.
927. Government could mobilise all privately owned Elkhounds for carrying military supplies over snow, in time of war.
928. Black East European Shepherd (developed from GSDs brought to Russia in the 1920's).
929. To promote the welfare and acceptance of the Dingo.

930. Australian Native Dog Training Society.
931. Danish Kennel Club.
932. Japanese Government. Reflected Japanese concern over the export and cross-breeding of native Japanese breeds. Declared all native breeds national monuments/treasures to provide official protection.
933. Music hall and stage animals who were forced to perform dangerous tricks, such as dogs thrown up into the air, spinning and then landing on one front leg.
934. Dogs' Home, Battersea.
935. Australian National Kennel Control.
936. Hound Trailing Association.
937. No. Only clubs and organisations can be members of the AKC.
938. Yes. Private members club, with no club or group membership.
939. Guide dogs for the blind movement.
940. 1993.
941. Annually.
942. Kennel Club of Japan.
943. 1928.
944. National Greyhound Racing Club.
945. United Kennel Club.
946. The Greyhound Hall of Fame.
947. 1912 (30 October).
948. United Kennel Club.
949. The official stud book.
950. 1905.
951. The Danish Kennel Club founded in 1897, the Norwegian Kennel Club was founded in 1898.
952. Individual membership, with individuals elected. after serving an apprentice period.
953. Ladies Kennel Association (LKA).
954. The Quaker Oats Company.

Section 3

955. a.   14th April 1949.
     b.   Royal Agricultural Society's Showground, during the

Royal Easter Show.

c.   Co-ordinating and recommendary body, not an overall controlling body such as the AKC or KC. Also maintains central register of prefixes.

956. Canberra Kennel Association.
Canine Association of Western Australia.
Canine Control Council (Queensland).
Kennel Control Council (Tasmania).
Kennel Control Council (Victoria).
Northern Australian Canine Association.
RAS Kennel Control, NSW.
South Australian Canine Association.

957.   All Breed; Obedience; Tracking.

958. a.   Waterloo Cup.
b.   Annual greyhound racing event held in February at Altcar.

959. a.   Bord na gCon.
b.   Tucson, Arizona.
c.   1951.

960. a.   American Veterinary Medical Association.
b.   UK – 1844; US – 1883.
c.   Professional governing bodies maintaining national registers of veterinarians.

961. a.   London 1978.
b.   30.
c.   Aimed to provide forum for the exchange of national views leading to closer understanding. Set tradition for future meetings.

962. a.   September 1982.
b.   American Kennel Club, New York.
c.   St Louis, Missouri.

963. a.   Rooms at the Philadelphia Kennel Club.

b. 14.

c. 1929 (Pure Bred Dogs. Title changed in 1938 to The Complete Dog Book).

964. a. London.
   b. 12.
   c. 1880.

965. a. 1974.
   b. 1899.
   c. 1978.

966. a. The film was called "221" (the street number of the AKC headquarters in New York at the time).
   b. A guide to the work of the AKC. Aimed at dog clubs and societies.
   c. AKC Librarian, Beatrice Peterson Agazzi.

967. Alaskan Malamute.
   American Foxhound.
   Beagle.
   Black 'n Tan Coonhound.
   Boston Terrier.
   Chesapeake Bay Retriever.
   Cocker Spaniel (American).
   Rough Collie.

968. a. 1880.
   b. 1889.
   c. American Field (originally called The Chicago Field).

969. a. Rescue dogs used during the London Blitz to find people trapped in the bombed buildings.
   b. Locating aircraft's black box flight recorders after a plane has crashed.
   c. Search dogs always wear a harness, patrol dogs wear a collar.

970. a. 1940
   b. German Shepherd Dogs

c.   All recruits originally pet dogs given as gifts from the general public.

971. a.   Royal Society for the Protection of the Animals (RSPCA.
b   Rev. Arthur Broome.
c.   Queen Victoria.

972. a.   Dogs for the Deaf.
b.   Claims the same access rights as guide dogs for the blind.
c.   Dogs have a blaze orange collar and lead. Owner carries photo I.D..

973. a.   Assistance Dogs and People Together.
b.   Assistance Dogs for the Disabled.
c.   SOHO Foundation.

974. a.   People's Dispensary for Sick Animals.
b.   Whitechapel, in the East End of London.
c.   To provide free treatment for sick animals if owners cannot afford private veterinary fees.

975. a.   The Blue Cross.
b.   Victoria, London.
c.   The League was very active in the 1st World War, caring for the thousands of animals used by the army. The logo was adopted to distinguish it from the Red Cross when working in the battlefields.

976. a.   Irish Coursing Club.
b.   15 September - 10 March.
c.   US - American National Waterloo Cup.

977. a.   Whippet Racing Association.
b.   Whippet Coursing Club.
c.   WRA races dogs registered by the Kennel Club competing on a standardized handicapping system of yard

per pound of weight. The WCC organized coursing races during the coursing season (September-March).

978   a.   John F Kennedy International Airport, New York.
     b.   Trained to sniff out prohibited produce or food, such as fresh fruit, meats, soil, plants and birds. The Beagles are not trained to sniff out drugs.
     c.   Beagle sniffs passengers' luggage, and if successful the dog is trained to give a passive response by sitting down next to and pointing to the passenger or their luggage.

Personalities Answers

Section 1

979. Louis Dobermann.
980. Elizabeth Barratt Browning.
981. Rev. John Russell known as Parson Jack Russell.
982. Well-known Cumberland huntsman who ran his own pack of hounds for over 40 years. Born in 1776 and died in 1854.
983. Charles Cruft.
984. King Canute.
985. St Bernard, who founded 2 hospices for travellers in the Swiss Alps, which became famous for using dogs (St Bernards) to rescue lost travellers.
986. Sewallis E Shirley.
987. James M Taylor.
988. Richard Gibson.
989. B G Jacobs.
990. Chauncy Z. Bennett.
991. General George Patton.
992. General Douglas MacArthur.
993. George, Lord Byron.
994. Adolf Hitler.
995. Laika.
996. Belka & Strelka.
997. Sir Walter Scott.
998. Alexandra, Princess of Wales, later Queen Alexandra.
999. James Watson, author of The Dog Book, 1905.
1000. Diogenes.
1001. $15 million.
1002. Duke of Gloucester.
1003. Cavalier King Charles Spaniel.
1004. King George VI and Queen Elizabeth.
1005. The World Cup Trophy, which had been stolen.
1006. Rats.
1007. Marjorie.
1008. Duke of Gordon.

Personalities Answers

1009. Ian Dunbar.
1010. Geraldine Rockefeller Dodge.
1011. Lucy Dawson.
1012. Phil Drabble.
1013. Thomas Fall.
1014. Sir Martin Frobisher and crew on his expedition searching for the North West Passage, 1577.
1015. King Charles II.
1016. Wally Herbert.
1017. 45.
1018. German Shepherd Dogs.
1019. Eadweard Muybridge.
1020. Ivan Pavlov.
1021. Master McGrath.
1022. Helen Keller.
1023. Thelma Gray.
1024. Count A P Hamilton.
1025. Puli.
1026. Sussex Spaniels.
1027. Jimmy or Jemmy Shaw.
1028. Basenji.
1029. Madame de Pompadour.
1030. Chinese Crested Dog.
1031. General George Custer.
1032. One of General Howe's foxhounds. It has strayed across into American lines, and was identified by the inscription on its collar.
1033. August Belmont, Jnr., President of the AKC.
1034. Spent 30 years as a dog food salesman for Spratts, ending up as General Manager.
1035. August Belmont, Jnr - 27 years.
1036. Duchess of Newcastle.
1037. American Pit Bull Terriers.
1038. President Eisenhower.
1039. Shannon, a Cocker Spaniel.
1040. She was the daughter of the Russian astronaut dog Strelka.
1041. President Johnson accepted the Collie as a gift from all the children of America.
1042. Checker was a black and white Cocker Spaniel, which the

Nixon family received as a present and kept as the family pet.

1043. Laekenois – Belgian Shepherd Dog.

1044. Blenheim Spaniel, variety of King Charles and Cavalier King Charles Spaniels, named after Blenheim Palace, home of Marlborough.

1045. Commodore Matthew Perry.

1046. Pyrenean Mountain Dog (Great Pyrenees).

1047. Great Dane.

1048. Kerry Blue Terrier.

1049. Afghan Hound.

1050. Colette.

1051. Jacqueline Susan.

1052. Rhodesian Ridgebacks.

1053. Bullmastiff.

1054. Captain G A Graham.

1055. Henry VIII.

1056. Roswell Eldridge, an American who on a visit to England in 1926, offered an annual prize for King Charles Spaniels at Crufts.

1057. King Edward VII.

1058. English Setter.

1059. Fox Terrier.

1060. Lord Lonsdale.

1061. Bill Cosby.

1062. James Hinks of Birmingham.

1063. O P Smith.

1064. Napoleon Bonaparte.

1065. Scottish Terrier.

1066. The German Shepherd was originally called Kiss, and Frank found this name too embarassing.

1067. Racing Greyhound, which won the Derby 2 consecutive times, and won 46 of out his 61 races.

1068. J Lloyd Price, of Rhiwlas, Bala, who organised the first trial in 1873.

1069. Carl Spitz.

1070. George Washington.

1071. King Charles I.

1072. Geoffrey Howe.

1073. Edward VIII, Duke of Windsor.
1074. Lady Kitty Ritson, who first introduced the breed into GB.
1075. Frank Jones, Whip to the Norwich Staghounds.
1076. Cecil Aldin.
1077. Labrador Retriever.

Section 2

1078. C Steadman Hanks, of the Seacroft Kennels.
1079. Fox Terrier.
1080. Howard Knight.
1081. Lord George Scott.
1082. Earl of Malmesbury.
1083. Theodore Roosevelt.
1084. Professor Raymond Triquet.
1085. Dr Antonio Nores Martinez, who wanted a tough guard-dog, but trustworthy family dog.
1086. Czesky Terriers.
1087. American hunter, who was one of the most successful promoters of the American Blue Gascon Hound. Wrote "Big 'N' Blue" short stories about the Old Line strain, and got the breed its nickname.
1088. Mrs Wingfield-Digby.
1089. William E Buckley, President of the AKC.
1090. Sigmund Freud.
1091. Hamish MacInnes, leader of Glencoe mountain rescue team.
1092. Mr & Mrs Milton Seeley.
1093. King Henry III.
1094. Badge worn by pilgrims to the Holy Land.
1095. Messr. Hickman and R Hood Wright.
1096. Sir John Buchanan-Jardine, Master of the Dumfriesshire Hounds.
1097. James Farrow.
1098. C A Phillips.
1099. Mrs Mary Amps.
1100. Major and Mrs Bell-Murray.
1101. Boughey family form Aqualate, Norfolk.
1102. The Clumber Spaniel was originally a French breed

developed by the Duc, who brought his kennels to Clumber Park, after he left France during the French Revolution.

1103. Gaston Pouchain, President of the French Kennel Club and the Brittany Spaniel Club of France.
1104. Cecil Moore.
1105. Earl of Malmesbury.
1106. Duke of Buccleuch.
1107. General Sir Douglas and Lady Brownrigg.
1108. William Arkwright.
1109. Duchess of Montrose.
1110. Newfoundland.
1111. 4 categories by colour: white, black, grey and yellow. Further divided by value and beauty.
1112. Physician in Chief to Queen Elizabeth I. Also co-founder of Caius College, Cambridge University.
1113. German Shorthaired Pointer.
1114. Captain John Edwards.
1115. Queen Victoria.
1116. Eurasier, or Eurasian dog.
1117. Irish Wolfhound, famous as a Red Cross dog during the 1st World War, who later shepherded sheep in Central Park, New York.
1118. Joseph Allen and Konrad Most.
1119. Harrison Weir.
1120. In 1894, J M Barrie married Mary Ansell, and on their honeymoon in Switzerland, they saw a litter of St Bernard puppies, and chose one.
1121. Gilbert White.
1122. R Lydekker.
1123. Konrad Lorenz.
1124. Major Herber.
1125. American Staffordshire Bull Terrier.
1126. Rodolphe Darzens.
1127. Mrs Raymond Mallock.
1128. King Henry IV's mistress, Corisande.
1129. Baron Freidrich von Steuben.
1130. Baron Georges Cuvier.
1131. King Henry VIII.

1132. King James I.
1133. Alexander Forbes of Aberdeen, 1617.
1134. Matthew Hopkins, the witchfinder general.
1135. Sir Edward Elgar.
1136. Sir Edward Elgar.
1137. All Base Section Commanders were to ensure that all pets at the army camps were not to be abandoned, and the Commanders were to liaise with the RSPCA.
1138. President of the FCI.
1139. Heinrich Essig.
1140. Robert Brooks.
1141. Charles Cruft.
1142. Lord Willoughby d'Eresly.
1143. Sir Everett Millais.
1144. Senator George Vest.
1145. Dr Rudolphina Menzel.
1146. Dr Henry Heimlich.
1147. Wing-Commander J A C and Mrs Ethnie Cecil-Wright.
1148. Group Captain "Beefy" and Mrs Catherine Sutton.
1149. J H Walsh.
1150. Rev. Thomas Pearce.
1151. Clifford Hubbard.
1152. Dr J Frank Perry.

Section 3

1153. Bijou.
1154. Greyfriars Bobby.
1155. Boatswain, Lord Byron's pet dog.
1156. Millie, George Bush's pet dog.
1157. Francis Redmond.
1158. Mrs W M Charlesworth.
1159. Sewallis E Shirley.
1160. Keeper, Emily and Charlotte Bronte's pet dog.
1161. Barry.
1162. Rin Tin Tin.
1163. Flush, Elizabeth Barratt Browning's pet dog.
1164. Lord Tweedmouth.
1165. Balthasar (John Galsworthy's Forsythe Saga).

1166. Rufus, Sir Winston Churchill's pet dog
1167. Snoopy

Section 4

1168. Basset Hound.
1169. Tibetan Terrier.
1170. Bullmastiff.
1171. Miniature Pinscher.
1172. Welsh Springer Spaniel.
1173. Soft Coated Wheaten Terrier.
1174. Pyrenean Mountain Dog.
1175. Pomeranian.
1176. Irish Setter.
1177. West Highland White Terrier.
1178. Airedale Terrier.
1179. Standard Poodle.
1180. St Bernard.
1181. French Bulldog.
1182. Japanese Chin.
1183. Hungarian Vizsla.
1184. Border Terrier.
1185. Borzoi.
1186. Miniature Schnauzer.
1187. Smooth Collie.
1188. Lowchen.
1189. Kerry Blue Terrier.
1190. Lakeland Terrier.
1191. Dalmatian.
1192. Whippet.
1193. Cocker Spaniel (American).
1194. Boston Terrier.
1195. Old English Sheepdog.
1196. Bouvier de Flandres.
1197. Cocker Spaniel (American).
1198. Clumber Spaniel.
1199. Bulldog.
1200. Boxer.
1201. Greyhound.

Personalities Answers

1202. Akita.
1203. American Water Spaniel.
1204. American Wirehaired Pointing Griffon.
1205. Bloodhound.
1206. Borzoi.
1207. Brussels Griffon.
1208. Chesapeake Bay Retriever.
1209. Collie.
1210. Corgi (Cardigan Welsh).
1211. Chow Chow.
1212. Briard.
1213. Bernese Mountain Dog.
1214. Australian Terrier.
1215. Brittany.
1216. Chinese Crested Dog.
1217. Afghan Hound.

Arts Answers

Section 1

1218. Sir Arthur Conan Doyle.
1219. Homeward Bound.
1220. Shadow.
1221. Perdita.
1222. Old English Sheepdog.
1223. Rulf.
1224. Nana.
1225. Killing a rat.
1226. Hounds.
1227. W C Fields.
1228. Noel Coward.
1229. Toby.
1230. George, Lord Byron.
1231. Bullet (Trigger was his horse).
1232. The Flight of the Navigator.
1233. Howliday Inn.
1234. Rudyard Kipling.
1235. Oliver Goldsmith.
1236. Lewis Carroll.
1237. A black dog.
1238. Death, or the appearance of spirits.
1239. Kiss a dog.
1240. Lares and his dog.
1241. Aleuts.
1242. 3-headed guardian dog of Hades, who was dragged into the daylight by Hercules.
1243. A thief.
1244. Eric Knight.
1245. Italian Greyhound.
1246. Robinson Crusoe.
1247. Walt Disney cartoon extra-terrestrial dogs, possessing magical powers who end up on earth and have to pretend to be normal dogs until they are helped to return to their own planet.

1248. "Doggone" Valentine.
1249. Waggles.
1250. Bulldog.
1251. The Family dog, 1987.
1252. The Beagles.
1253. Spike, the Bulldog.
1254. Fox.
1255. Richard Adams.
1256. All dogs go to heaven (1989).
1257. The fox and the hound (1981).
1258. Silver Blaze, in the "Memoirs of Sherlock Holmes".
1259. Hounds.
1260. Talbot Hound.
1261. Hound on scent.
1262. Left the King's side, and attached itself to his enemy ,Henry of Lancaster.
1263. Hunting and hawking.
1264. Column of Marcus Aurelius.
1265. Hottest part of the summer (July-August) when Sirius, the dog star rises at dawn.
1266. St Bernard.
1267. Sir Percy Fitzpatrick.
1268. J F Herring.
1269. Weston Bell.
1270. 1970, coinciding with Expo '70 in Osaka.
1271. His Master's Voice.
1272. Toby, his Setter ate it.
1273. Hart to Hart.
1274. Napoleon.
1275. Patti Page.
1276. Diamond Dogs.
1277. Cat Stevens.
1278. Flanagan & Hall.
1279. Bonzo Dog Doo-Da Band.
1280. Snoop Doggy Dogg.
1281. Spike.
1282. Ralph.
1283. Old Mother Hubbard, by Sarah Catherine Martin.
1284. Troy.

1285. Newfoundland.
1286. John Galsworthy.
1287. Alexander Pope.
1288. Ogden Nash.
1289. George Bernard Shaw.
1290. Abbotsford.
1291. Ecclesiastes (IX, 4).
1292. Actaeon, the hunter.
1293. Dogs, horses and mules.
1294. Celestial dog of Chinese mythology.
1295. Pat.
1296. Laurel and Hardy's mongrel.
1297. Scraps.
1298. Dr Snuggles.
1299. Rude Dog and the Dweebs.
1300. Mississippi.
1301. No.
1302. Davey and Goliath.
1303. Translucent/invisible dog belonging to Jack Skellington, the Pumpkin King.
1304. Root Bolton.
1305. Tackhammer.
1306. Bob.
1307. Bob Carolgees.
1308. Jumble.
1309. Bruno.
1310. Mr Peabody.
1311. Scruffy.

Section 2

1312. John Heywood.
1313. Nathan Bailey.
1314. Mark Twain.
1315. Poodle.
1316. Airedale Terrier.
1317. Jean Cocteau.
1318. Sammy (short for Sampson), the Bull Terrier.
1319. Jerome K Jerome's Novel notes, 1893.

1320. Venérie de Jacques du Fouilloux, 1585.

1321. Dame Juliana Berners' "The Boke of St Albans", 1486.

1322. Thomas Brown's "Biographical sketches and authentic anecdotes of dogs, 1829.

1323. Thomas Carlye.

1324. Robert Scanlan's "My book of curs", 1840.

1325. Chapman Pincher.

1326. Baudelaire.

1327. Duke.

1328. P G Wodehouse's Jeeves.

1329. Emily Dickinson.

1330. Karel Capek.

1331. Dorothy Parker.

1332. John Steinbeck.

1333. To do what he wanted for one day, because all his life he had had to be good.

1334. Jeroslav Hasek's "The good soldier Svejk".

1335. Jack London's "The Call of the Wild".

1336. Samuel Pepys.

1337. Lord Macaulay.

1338. John Galsworthy's "The Silver Spoon" (part of the Forsythe Saga).

1339. Shoscombe Old Place.

1340. Strabo.

1341. War dogs, trained to fight in platoons, and used in the Roman army's front line.

1342. Greyhound.

1343. The Wife of Bath's prologue.

1344. Samuel Johnson.

1345. Caper (half Newfoundland, half Spaniel).

1346. George Elliot.

1347. John Dryden.

1348. Pug (Spectre of Tappington, Inglesby Legends).

1349. Elizabeth Barratt and Robert Browning.

1350. Miguel de Cervantes.

1351. Woodrow Wilson.

1352. The Merchant of Venice (Act 3, scene 3).

1353. Midsummer's Night Dream.

1354. Henry V (Act 2, scene 1).

1355. Henry IV Part 2 (Act 2, scene 4).
1356. Henry v (Act 3, scene 7).
1357. Julius Caesar Act 3, scene 1).
1358. Legend says that the Bishop Godfrey's hound deliberately ate a poisoned dish of food intended for his master.
1359. Saint Roche, patron saint of dogs, and whose protection is sought against rabies and the plague.
1360. Hounds were taken up to the church alter and fed cake. This provided protection against rabies throughout the year
1361. Keeping any greyhound or other dog for hunting.
1362. Wolves.
1363. Disrupted church services by barking, and sometimes tore up church books.
1364. Odysseus's dog, who still recognised his master when he returned in disguise after 19 years. Argus died from the joy of seeing Odysseus again.
1365. Pattern designed by the culture hero Maui, when he tattooed a dog's muzzle black.
1366. The cat wins the race by reaching home first, and so he is allowed to live indoors, while the dog must keep watch from outside.
1367. a. The dog helped Noah drive all the animals aboard the Ark and was the last animal to go aboard. There was no room for him inside, and so the dog spent 40 days with his nose in the rain.
b. The Ark sprang a leak, and the dog stopped the hole with his nose.
1368. Dogs were scavengers and ate the flesh of animals which were regarded as forbidden and unclean. Also associated with pagan idolatry.
1369. Family shaved themsleves as a symbol of deep mourning.
1370. Signalled the annual flooding of the Nile, and the need to move cattle to higher ground.
1371. Allbe, King Mesroda' of Leinster's hound.
1372. True.
1373. Anubis, the jackal-headed god of the death.
1374. Frighten away death. Also incarnation of the God Bhaironath.
1375. Their fingernails.

1376. Sicily.
1377. Reincarnated lamas punished for their faithlessness.
1378. Corpse-eating/pariah dogs.
1379. Kato Indians of California.
1380. Sent to the underworld to bring back the bones of the ancestors so that the first human pair could be created.
1381. Glen of Imaal Terrier.
1382. Pack of spectral hounds, often headless, and thought to be the spirits of unbaptised children, who roam through forests and woodland at night.
1383. Prince Rupert of the Rhine's poodle called Boye.
1384. Spectral hound said to haunt Peel Castle on the Isle of Man
1385. The 2-headed dog that guarded the red cattle of Geryon. Hercules's 10th task was to slay him.
1386. Alaunt.
1387. Simon de Monfort.
1388. Bloodhound and Scottish Terrier.
1389. Sir Edwin Landseer.
1390. Maud Earl.
1391. A hound.
1392. Sitting on the table next to the Duke.
1393. Relieving itself against one of the stable posts.
1394. Bonzo, by George Studdy.
1395. Alexandre-Francois Desportes.
1396. Thomas Gainsborough.
1397. Sir Edwin Landseer.
1398. French Bulldog, called Bouboule.
1399. Archie and Amos.
1400. Dog barking at the Moon.
1401. Max.
1402. Huckleberry Hound.
1403. True.
1404. Joseph Tabrar, sung by Miss Vesta Victoria.
1405. Most of Nimo's tricks were done without the handler being on the stage.
1406. Franklin D. Roosevelt (relating to his Scottish Terrier, Fala).
1407. The Dogfather, by Fritz Freling.
1408. Weakheart.

1409. Ralph Wolf and Sam Sheepdog
1410. Symbol of the devotion of dog in the service of man, commemorating the 1925 rescue sled drive 340 miles from Nenana to Nome. Diphtheria had broken out in Nome, and bad weather made transporting the medical serum immpossible apart from dog sled
1411. Early English period (c.1189-1307)

Section 3

1412. a. Samuel Pepys.
    b. King Charles II.
    c. Toy Spaniels (King Charles and Cavalier King Charles Spaniels).

1413. a. Montmorency.
    c. Jermone K Jerome.
    c. No.

1414. a. P G Wodehouse's character Uckridge.
    b. Training dogs for the music-hall stage.
    c. 6 Pekingese.

1415. a. Dr Watson does not know why he was sent to 3 Pinchin Lane, and just knows that he must get Toby!
    b. Sherlock Holmes.
    c. A mongrel. Half Spaniel, half lurcher which was used as a tracking dog to hunt for the murderers of Major Sholto.

1416. a. Part Bloodhound, part Mastiff.
    b. Bought from Ross and Mangles in Fulham, London.
    c. Island on Grimpen Mire.

1417. a. John Galsworthy in "The silver spoon" (Forsythe Saga).
    b. Dandie Dinmont and a Pekingese.
    c. Soames Forsyth.e

1418. a. John Galsworthy in "The Silver Spoon" (Forsythe Saga).

    b. Dandie Dinmont.

    c. Fleur Mont.

1419. a. Cecile Aubrey.

    b. French Pyrenees.

    c. Pyreneean Mountain Dog.

1420. a. Mr and Mrs Dearley.

    b. Cruella De Vil, Jasper and Horace.

    c. Make a fur coat out of the puppy skins.

1421. a. Dodie Smith.

    b. The Starlight barking: more about the 101 Dalmatians.

    c. Sirius, the Dog Star cast a spell over the whole world, and wanted to take all the dogs to be with him on the lonely star.

1422. a Alfred Bestall.

    b. Pong-Ping, the Pekingese; Algy, the Pug.

1423. a. 12.

    b. Live and let live.

    c. Deceit deserves to be deceived.

1424. a. Woof.

    b. Allan Ahlbery.

    c. Norfolk Terrier.

1425. a. Fictional Liddesdale farmer in Sir Walter Scott's "Guy Mannering" who owned a special breed of terrier.

    b. Mustard and Pepper according to their colour, with no other distinction apart from such adjectives as "Young", "Old" or "Little".

    c. James Davidson of Hindlee.

1426. a. The New Yorker.

    b. 1943.

    c. "Is sex necessary", 1929. Written with E B White as co-author.

1427. a. George Elliot's "Middlemarch".
      b. St Bernard called Monk.

1428. a. Labes, tried for stealing a cheese.
      b. Alcibiades was an ancient Athenian General. Reputedly cut off his dog's tail in an attempt to distract the Athenians from his tyranny by such an act of eccentricity.
      c. Laelaps.

1429. a. I Kings 21:23.
      b. Matthew 15:27.
      c. The Song of Solomon 2:15.

1430. a. Florence Dombey – Dombey and Son.
      b. Mr Jingles – The Pickwick Papers.
      c. Dora Spenlow (later Copperfield) – David Copperfield.

1431. a. James Joyce's "Ulysses".
      b. G K Chesterton's "The Flying Inn".
      c. Charlotte Bronte's "Shirley".

1432. a. Ambrose Bierce "The enlarged devil's dictionary".
      b. Lilies in the field (Matthew 6:28).
      c. "Lowest rank in the hierarchy of dogs".

1433. a. Edward, 2nd Duke of York's manuscript "The master of game", 1406-13.
      b. Limited edition published in 1906.
      c. Sydenham Edward's Cynographia Britannica, 1800.

1434. a. W H Auden (In Memory of Sigmund Freud).
      b. Federico Garcia Lorca (Ballard of the Spanish Civil War).
   c.   Ogden Nash (An Introduction to Dogs).

1435. a. Douglas Jerrold.
      b. William Penn.
      c. John B Bogart.

1436. a. Lion, dog and horse.

b. Scavenger dogs which ate corpses, and howled at the Moon.

c. Whelping bitch.

1437. a. Prince Llewellyn ap Joweth was out hunting, and returned to find his faithful hound Gelert covered in blood. His infant son's cradle was overturned and Llewellyn jumped to the conclusion that Gelert had attached and killed the baby. In his fury, he killed the dog, only to discover that Gelert had defended and killed a wolf that had attacked the baby, which was still alive.

b. Allegedly, King John gave the dog to Llewellyn.

c. Beddgelert, in Snowdonia.

1438. a. King Arthur's dog Cabal.

b. Cornwall.

c. Arthur's Troughs.

1439. a. Originally known as Culain, he was renamed Cuchulain after slaying the Great Smith of Ulster's watchdog. His name means Hound of Culain, and he was also known as the Hound of Ulster.

b. He could not eat dog flesh.

c. He took over the guarding duties of the watchdog he had killed.

1440. a. Odin, also known as Woden the Storm-God.

b. A spectral pack of hounds and huntsmen led by Woden who rode nightly in pursuit of a phantom boar, horse or woman.

c. A hound left on a hearth lived on ashes, howling and whining for a year.

1441. a. 7 swift hounds from Sparta.

b. The crowning of dogs with hawthorn to protect the dogs from the avenging spirits of wild animals they had killed.

c. Diana.

1442. a. The last sheaf.
    b. Killed the dog of the harvest.
    c. The Bitch.

1443. Cabilon, Lubina and Melampo.

1444. a. Guard-dog against stranger and burglars, but also protected the home against demons and evil spirits.
    b. A mosaic or painting of a chained dog, with the inscription "cave canem".
    c. Beware of the dog.

1445. a. Meissen.
    b. Rockingham.
    c. Royal Worcester.

1446. a. Weimaraner called Man Ray.
    b. Weimaraner called Fay Ray.

1447. a. William Hogarth.
    b. Trump.
    c. Tate Gallery, London.

1448. a. George Studd.y
    b. Yes.
    c. 1924.

1449. a. All of them.
    b. Yes.
    c. Friendship, protection and justice.

1450. a. Obelix.
    b. Dogmatix.
    c. Idefix.

1451. a. Asta.
    b. Schnauzer.
    c. Wirehaired Fox Terrier.

1452. a. Dorothy's dog in L Frank Braum's "The Wizard of Oz".
b. Cairn Terrier.
c. Border Terrier (Return to Oz).

1453. a. French Poodle.
b. Bimbo the dog, and Ko-Ko the clown.

1454. a. Mark Twain's book "Roughing it", with its descriptions of coyotes and jackrabbits. Also Aesop's fable of the fox and the grapes.
b. Always from the coyote's viewpoint.
c. Never injures the roadrunner.

1455. a. Cartoon dog, who has ghost-hunting adventures.
b. Great Dane.
c. Scrappy-Doo.

1456. a. American Cocker spaniel.
b. Jock.
c. Blodhound.

1457. a. Glacier National Park, Montana, USA.
b. New Mexico.
c. King Edward III kenneled his greyhounds there.

1458. a. Pug.
b. Her father, Lucian Freud.
c. Trussardi.

1459. a. Petra, the Blue Peter dog.
b. 1962.
c. Shep, the Border Collie.

1460. a. Dogs and hunting.
b. 2nd November.
c. Against hunting injuries and rabies.

1461. a. The magic transformation of a man into a dog, or dog into the human form, or a form of insanity in which a person believes himself to be a dog.
b. Transformation of human into wolf, or werewolves.

1462. a. War and peace.
b. Siegfreid Sassoon.
c. George Earl.

1463. a. Dogue de Bordeaux.
b. German Shepherd Dog.
c. Jack Russell Terrier.

1464. a. Shadow.
b. Buster.
c. Scamp.

1465. a. Eric Hill.
b. Maurice Sendak.
c. Afghan Hound.

Picture Answers

1466. The height of a dog is measured from the ground to the withers (shoulder). See illustration below.
1467. The length of a dog is measured from the point of the shoulder to the point of the buttocks. See illustration below.

Feet

1468.	c.
1469.	b.
1470.	d.
1471.	a.

Profiles

1472.	a.
1473.	f.
1474.	c.
1475.	b.
1476.	e.
1477.	d.

Ears

1478.	d.
1479.	b.
1480.	c.
1481.	a.
1482.	f.
1483.	e.

Fronts

1484.	d.
1485.	a.
1486.	c.
1487.	f.
1488.	g.
1489.	e.
1490.	b.

Tails

1491.	c.
1492.	e.
1493.	f.
1494.	g.
1495.	a.
1496.	b.
1497.	j.
1498.	l.
1499.	i.
1500.	k.
1501.	h.
1502.	d.

QUESTION

"Where can I buy the best books available on my favourite dog breeds?"